ANKFURT

# THE NEW GUIDE
# Michael's

## FRANKFURT

Managing Editor
**Michael Shichor**

Series Editor
**Amir Shichor**

*INBAL TRAVEL INFORMATION LTD.*

Inbal Travel Information Ltd.
P.O.Box 1870 Ramat Gan 52117
Israel

**Intl. ISBN 965-288-126-0**

Graphic design: Michel Opatowski
Cover design: Bill Stone
Photography: Stadt Frankfurt am Main – Tourist Board,
             Amir Shichor, Sharon Bentov, Yossi Shrem
Photo editor: Shmulik Weiss
Editorial: Ofer Wasserman, Sharona Johan
D.T.P.: Irit Bahalul
Printed by Havatzelet Press Ltd.

**Sales in the UK
and Europe:**
Kuperard (London) Ltd.
9 Hampstead West
224 Iverson Road
London NW6 2HL

**Distribution in the UK
and Europe:**
Bailey Distribution Ltd.
Learoyd Road
New Romney
Kent TN28 8X

**U.K. ISBN 1-85733-124-9**

# CONTENTS

## INTRODUCTION

## FRANKFURT

# TABLE OF MAPS

## Preface

Frankfurt is a cosmopolitan city, a city of business. It is the financial heart of Germany and the home of most major international banks. The city is historically renowned as a site for international trade fairs, which have been held there since the thirteenth century. Frankfurt's international ambience is also manifested in the many languages spoken throughout the city.

But there is more to this wonderful city than business. The Frankfurters work hard and play hard, and opportunities for entertainment and leisure are plentiful. Concerts, theater, pubs and restaurants are an integral part of Frankfurt's night life. The street scene is lively, as outdoor fruit-and-vegetable vendors hawk their wares, and bands play in the open squares. Along the Zeil, street musicians and roving puppeteers claim a bit of ground and crowds circle around to watch. When it rains, they take refuge in one of the underground shopping passages. There, too, one finds sidewalk artists copying the *Mona Lisa* or Garfield cartoons.

The city is also blessed with beautiful parks and forests, and at the first sign of sun these fill up with locals and tourists alike.

Frankfurt has, regretfully, been a most neglected city by tourists. We hope to give you a better understanding of Frankfurt and reveal to you the special charm of this city. We want to lead you to its most exciting attractions, and to ensure that you make the most of your stay in Frankfurt. We are sure that the effort invested in compiling this guide will be justified and that your trip will remain a wonderful memory for days to come.

Michael Shichor

## Using this Guide

In order to reap maximum benefit from the information in this guide, we advise the traveler to carefully read the following passage. The facts contained in this book were compiled to help the tourist find his or her way around and to ensure that he enjoys his stay to the upmost.

The "Introduction" provides details which will help you make the early decisions and arrangements for your trip. We suggest that you carefully review the material, so that you will be more organized and set for your visit. Upon arrival in Frankfurt, you will feel familiar and comfortable with the city.

The tour routes, laid out geographically, lead the visitor up and down the city's streets, providing a survey of the sites and calling attention to all those details which deepen one's familiarity with Frankfurt, and make a visit there so much more enjoyable.

The reader will notice that certain facts tend to recur. This is deliberate; it enables the tourist who starts out from a point other than the one we choose to be no less informed. The result is a flexibility in personal planning.

Following the tour routes, we have included a selection of "Day Trips", which are all extremely interesting. Each of these excursions makes for a very pleasant trip out of the city.

The rich collection of maps covers the tour routes and special attractions in great detail. Especially prepared for this book, they will certainly add to the efficiency and pleasure of your exploration of Frankfurt.

A concise list of "Musts" follows, describing those sites without which your visit is not complete.

Since Frankfurt is highly esteemed for its cuisine, shopping and entertainment, a special chapter is devoted to "Making the Most of your Stay" in the city. Here you will find a broad range of possibilities to suit your budget, needs and tastes.

As most tourists arriving in Frankfurt are not familiar with the German language, we have added a short vocabulary containing some basic words; these may help you while traveling around the country.

To further facilitate the use of this guide, we have included a detailed index. It includes all the major sites mentioned throughout the book. Consult the index to find something by name and it will refer you to the place where it is mentioned in greatest detail.

Because times and cities are dynamic, an important rule of thumb when traveling, and especially when visiting a vibrant city like Frankfurt, should be to consult local sources of information. Tourists are liable to encounter certain inaccuracies in this guide, and for this we apologize.

In this guide we have tried to present updated information in a way which allows for an easy, safe and economical visit. For this purpose, we have included a short questionnaire and will be most grateful for those who will take the time to complete it and send it to us.

Have a pleasant and exciting trip – Bon Voyage!

# PART ONE – AN OVERVIEW

Frankfurt means business. It is the commercial capital of Germany, its banking and stock trading center, and to a great extent it affects the economic pulse of both Europe and the rest of the world. Among its hundreds of banking concerns are firms from America, Australia, Japan, and Hong Kong, and it is also the headquarters for the powerful *Bundesbank* (German Central Bank).

The Frankfurt Stock Exchange deals in billions of Deutsche Mark (DM) every year, and the Currency Exchange is an influential world money market. The Zeil, the town's most prosperous shopping street, is an international wholesale and retail center. The city's Frankfurter *Messe* (fairgrounds) has gained significant international attention as a site for exhibitions on the latest technological and consumer goods. Frankfurt has, in fact, a history of hosting important trade fairs since the thirteenth century.

Frankfurt is literally situated at the crossroads of Europe, where eight-lane, speed-unlimited *Autobahnen* (superhighways) fan out toward all major European capitals. The airport is the busiest on the Continent, with take offs or landings almost every minute. The main railway station is the most active passenger station in Europe, shuttling 1500 trains in and out of the city every day. The port offers easy access to the Rhine, Europe's workhorse river.

The city has also begun to make its mark as a political entity, even though it is neither the political capital of the country nor the capital of its own state, Hesse. Dozens of countries staff consulates in Frankfurt. Frankfurt has a distinct sense of tradition, and is very active in the fields of art and culture.

In spite of all this, Frankfurt has, remarkably, not made it as a tourist center. Tourists who are in the area spend very little time in the city, and those who do stay in Frankfurt are often too busy doing business to enjoy the city.

INTRODUCTION

This is unfortunate. With a population of about 635,000, Frankfurt is small enough to be hospitable, and large enough to be sophisticated. Except for the somewhat confusing one-way streets, it is remarkably easy to get around town. Walking is popular on pleasant days because of easy access to most places. The public transportation network is fast and convenient. The cream-colored taxi fleet – consisting mostly of Mercedes cars – is efficient, and chauffeured limousines are readily available.

A final word: Frankfurt is generally referred to by its full name, Frankfurt am Main (Frankfurt on the Main River), to distinguish it from Frankfurt an der Oder, in what used to be East Germany. The name is usually abbreviated to Frankfurt a.M.

## A Capsule History

Frankfurt is a city of the future, but it is firmly rooted in its past. The city was a Free Imperial City until 1866, liberal stronghold of the bourgeois, coronation city of the Emperors of the Holy Roman Empire of the German Nation, and trade center during the Middle Ages.

It owes its existence to a narrow crossing point on the River Main, from which it derived its name – the Frank's Ford. A settlement sprang up long before the Franks arrived, however, and traces of Late Stone Age peoples were uncovered when the Eastern Harbor was built. The Romans built a bridge and a fort here in the first century AD. The tribes that followed – the Celts, the Allemani and the Franks – then settled the site.

Charlemagne made the earliest documented mention of a place called Franconofurd in 793AD, referring to the little hill now known as the Römerberg. Here he built a fortification near the river and established a royal palace.

The palace stood at the top of the hill, between where the Cathedral and the Römer (city hall) now stand. Around it the market-place sprang up and the merchants and patricians built shop-houses. The facilities were constructed for com-

*Medieval buildings at the Römerberg*

merce, with large cellars, wide halls and cranes attached at the fronts for unloading heavy goods.

Active trade led to the development of the Frankfurt Fair, which was first mentioned in 1240 and which blossomed in the 14th and 15th centuries. It is the predecessor of the International Frankfurt Autumn Fair, now held at the city fairgrounds. The Spring Fair is a younger offshoot which did not begin until 1330.

In 1405 the Town Council bought two of the shop-houses, the Römer and the Goldener Schwan, and converted them into the City Hall, which was later expanded to incorporate neighboring houses.

In 1562, Emperor Maximilian II moved the coronation center of the Holy Roman Empire from Aachen to Frankfurt, making the Römerberg the scene of sumptuous festivities that surpassed anything previously known.

In 1585, when Frankfurt was granted the right to mint coins, the German *Börse* (exchange) was established. In the middle of the century, sometime after the printer Christian Egenolff followed Johannes Gutenberg (the inventor of movable type) to Frankfurt, the city's first newspaper was being printed.

The Reich came to an end in 1806, and for a few years the city suffered political unstability. In 1815, with the establishment of the German Confederation, the Congress of Vienna declared Frankfurt an independent city and the seat of the Assembly of the Confederation (the Bundestag).

In 1848 the first German National Assembly met in

# INTRODUCTION

the Church of St. Paul (Pauluskirche) to formulate a constitution for a united Germany. Such democratic stirrings, which were part of the wave of revolutionary liberalism that swept Europe, did not please the Prussian king, Frederik William IV, even though he was offered the crown; in 1866, Prussian troops occupied the city and abolished its Free Imperial City status.

Nevertheless, business continued to flourish and soon banking houses were founded, many of which remain to this day. (The first of the Rothschild banks was established here in 1798, and the sons of the house went on to found banks in London, Paris, Naples and Vienna.)

Industry developed along the banks. In 1863 a dye factory was founded, and later expanded into pharmaceutical and photographic products, taking its name from the picturesque village Höchst. The firm is one of the powerhouses of the city's prosperity today.

From the mid eighteenth century many villas and garden houses were built along the roads radiating out of the city. Less wealthy citizens lived in apartments, constructed between the villas. These suburbs were in the course of time incorporated into the city.

Until the First World War, Frankfurt's development was controlled mainly by private persons, but in the twentieth century the city authorities took charge in order to plan more effectively.

During the Second World War, on March 22-23, 1944, the lovely heart of the city – the largest of Germany's surviving medieval cities – was destroyed in an air raid. On

*Modern skyscrapers rise behind medieval Frankfurt*

March 26, 1945, the American troops entered the city.

Unlike some German cities whose centers were rebuilt to replicate their originals, Frankfurt chose concrete and glass to start anew. Traces of the old days remain in some half-timbered houses and in four fifteenth-century towers, but they are almost hidden among the glittering skyscrapers.

## Topography

Frankfurt is situated in the valley of the Main River, shielded from Arctic blasts by the Taunus Range, which can be seen on a clear day from the city's taller buildings.

Although the original town lay on the north bank of the Main, the river now cuts a swath through the incorporated area. The city has grown to include the following surrounding villages, which still retain their names and distinct character: Sachsenhausen, Bornheim, Bockenheim, Seckbach, Bonames, Bergen-Enkheim.

Frankfurt's waterfront, the Main, stretches 25 kilometers (15.5 miles) from Fenchenheim to Sindlingen and includes two major harbors. The river is crossed by automobile, railway and pedestrian bridges.

The city is almost square in shape, 23.4 kilometers (14.5

miles) from east to west and 23.3 kilometers from north to south. It is a surprisingly large agricultural city, with some 7,000 hectares (2,834 acres) of cultivated land, much in small private holdings. It has 4,154 hectares (1,682 acres) of forests, of which the citizens are very proud. In fact, a special national holiday – *Waldtag* (Forest Day) – is celebrated each year to commemorate the city's lush surroundings. On this day businesses close and everyone travels to the woods to enjoy the greenery.

The city is bounded in the north by the little River Nidda and on the south by the *Stadtwald* (City Forest), a part of Sachsenhausen that encompasses the airport. The site was the first place in Europe where trees were planted from seed. In 1398 oaks were sown. Some of these huge old trees (marked with plaques) still stand. The area is criss-crossed with walking and bridle paths, and pleasant restaurants for the hungry or thirsty wanderer. When a new runway for the airport encroached upon this woodland, there was a strong protest from the residents. Grandmothers joined their long-haired progeny in demonstrations that sometimes resulted in pitched battles with the police.

## Climate

Frankfurt is low-lying, with its highest point at 212 meters, (695 feet) above sea level, and it is protected from north winds. As such, its winters tend to be wet but not really icy. It snows, but the snow soon turns to a brown slush and gurgles down the gutters. Smog can often be a problem.

January and February are the bitterest months, when the average temperature hovers around freezing. Spring arrives relatively early in Germany. It is heralded by yellow bursts of forsythia and a week or two of warm sunshine as early as the end of April. This is often a false promise, however, and cold weather can sometimes linger well into June. Although temperatures in July and

*The Deutsche Bank*

August average at about 18 degrees centigrade (65 degrees fahrenheit), the nights can be cool. Days may start out warm and sunny, only to dissolve into grey skies or showers.

Autumn is the best season to visit, as it is usually sunny and warm. Restaurants and cafes often keep their sidewalk tables out throughout this season, or until the November chill becomes too bitter.

Like most Germans, the Frankfurters love fresh air and keep their windows open a crack even in the middle of winter. In some buildings, the heating is turned off in April and not turned on again until November. To counter the cold, many hotels provide deliciously warm down quilts for their chilly clientele. The climate makes air-conditioning unnecessary, except during the most unusually hot summers. You will also find it in congress centers and entertainment halls where large crowds gather.

*The Messeturm, an important international trade center*

## Frankfurt – A Successful City

Frankfurt has a liberal tradition and culture that has kept pace with business. Art and cultural projects are frequently sponsored by business enterprises. In addition, Frankfurt has the largest budget set aside for cultural activities of any German city, supporting not only three theater production companies, but also a number of free theater groups, actors' groups and cabarets, as well as the city's museums and libraries.

The arts, some say, are as controversial as politics and are thoroughly interwoven. When the *Alte Oper* (Old Opera House) was being rebuilt in the late 1970s, the public demanded more than a showcase that only the rich could afford to visit. As a result, the building was redesigned as a concert and congress center where several events could be staged at the same time.

Goethe is without a doubt the

city's favorite cultural figure, though another writer, Dr. Heinrich Hoffmann, creator of the children's character Struwwelpeter, is also well loved.

Any day on the streets of Frankfurt, one can hear a dozen languages, see shop and hotel signs in Turkish or Japanese – and not just for the benefit of visitors. The population includes 150,000 foreigners in the diplomatic and business communities, and groups of *Gastarbeiter* (guest workers) who were inspired to work here during the boom of the 1960s and '70s. However, in the face of economic belt-tightening seen in the 1980s and '90s, in particular after the unification of both parts of Germany and the rise in unemployment, the country has seen mounting feelings against these guest workers.

# PART TWO – SETTING OUT

## Things you must know

Frankfurt has earned the dubious distinction of being the crime capital of Germany, primarily because all arrests at the airport are included in the city statistics. Yet in comparison with cities in the United States or England, it is remarkably safe.

Visitors should take the usual precautions, such as not leaving valuables in parked cars or lying about in hotel rooms. You should not flash large sums of money, and avoid dimly lit back streets at night. The railway stations and some of the parks are the haunts of the homeless and are ideal places for muggings. At night, the district of the Central Railway Station at Kaiserstraße is quite unpleasant.

The city is well-patrolled, and the visitor should have no fear about exploring Frankfurt freely.

During the large trade fairs, hotels raise their prices by 20 percent, and are fully booked. Determine in advance from your tourist office if hotels are likely to be booked when you plan your visit and make reservations accordingly. It is also a good idea to note the holidays, especially if you are on a business trip. Offices and shops are closed during Germany's many holidays (see "When to come; national holidays".)

## How to get there

**By air:** Frankfurt's Rhine-Main Airport, Germany's largest, lies about 10 kilometers from the city center. It is served by approximately 70 airlines, flying scheduled services. Many charter companies also use this airport as well. There is easy access from the airport to the city (see "Transportation").

**By rail:** Frankfurt central railway station, the *Hauptbahnhof*, is one of the largest and busiest railway stations in Europe. It is an important junction for both international and domestic traffic. About 1500 trains arrive at or depart from the station daily (see "Transportation").

**By bus:** *Europabus*, the regularly-scheduled bus network that criss-crosses the Continent, connects Frankfurt with about 200 cities in Europe. The German buses are easily recog-

nizable by their *Touring* logo, but buses from many countries make up the network. There are direct buses between Frankfurt and Lyon/Barcelona, and connections to Amsterdam, Paris, London, Warsaw, Antwerp and many other cities.

**By car:** Frankfurt is situated at a main traffic junction where *Autobahnen* 5 and 3 cross. There is easy access to the city by road, as it has links with the whole German and European motorway system.

**By ship:** From Easter to mid-October Frankfurt is served by ships of the *KD German Rhine Line.* A tunnel that opened in 1992 connects the Main and the Danube in Bavaria, facilitating direct passage between Eastern and Western Europe, from the Black Sea to the North Sea.

The landing stage and ticket pavilion are on the Mainkai at the Eiserner Steg. Combination ship/rail tickets are available for round trips. At Mainz, where the Main River joins the Rhine, you can change Lines, going north to Rotterdam or south to Basel.

## Documents and Customs Regulations

Customs checks are usually cursory at Germany's gateways. There is no limit to the amount of currency you can take in or out of the country. Non-European residents are allowed to bring in duty-free 400 cigarettes or 100 cigars or 500 grams tobacco; one liter of spirits and two liters of wine and 50 grams of perfume. (Smokers would be well advised to bring cigarettes, as they are very expensive in Germany). European residents are allowed fewer cigarettes, and the quantities of other items they can bring in duty-free also vary.

Customs officers tend to stop passengers arriving on flights from North Africa and the Middle East, but even so, it is usually a spot check. Travelers must pass through customs when they leave the International Transit Hall and again when they leave International Baggage Claim.

Customs and passport formalities are taken care of on board trains. Buses and cars stop at well-marked highway border crossings.

Visas for tourist visits of up to three month are not required by Germany for citizens of the United States, Great Britain, Canada, New Zealand, Australia, and other western countries.

If you plan to drive, you should have an International Drivers License. Ask your automobile club for assistance in obtaining a license.

Students should bring along a student ID card or an International Student Card for reductions in entry fees at museums and the like.

## INSURANCE

Health care in Germany is socialized, and most people who live there are covered through a health-insurance plan to which they and their employers contribute. Visitors will be considered private patients and will be expected to pay in cash. However, citizens of Great Britain can claim medical expenses through their own medical system. Before making a trip, get form E111 from the Department of Health and Social Security. Before going to a doctor in Germany, get an official paper from the *Allgemeine Ortskrankenkassen* (AOK), the National health authority.

If you purchase a travel insurance policy, find out what papers you need for making claims. Translations may be required.

*American Express* offers a medical and legal referral service, called Global Assist, to its Gold Card members without additional charge.

It is advisable to insure all your baggage and personal valuables against theft. Theft

among tourists is not rampant but has been known to occur. Do not take unneccessary chances.

## When to come; national holidays

Frankfurt has no big tourist season, but is most crowded during its trade fairs. Find out from your local tourist office when the fairs are scheduled to avoid this busy, high-priced time. Summer and the Christmas season are excellent times for tourists.

If your reason for coming to Frankfurt is a trade fair, be sure to plan ahead. Book a room well in advance. The *Messe Frankfurt GmbH* (Fair Association) books rooms during fairs for participants only. Contact the Messe, Torhaus Service Center, 1 Ludwig-Erhard-Anlage, Frankfurt a.M., D-60327, Tel. 75756222 or 75756695.

Making a suggestion about the season to visit Frankfurt is difficult, for summers can be cool and damp. However, from April through October, one can count on some pleasant weather. The city blossoms from about Easter until June, and the forests begin to change to autumn hues in late August. Always be prepared for rain.

Below is a list of the major holidays celebrated in Frankfurt.

1st January – New Year's Day
Easter Period –
 Shrove Tuesday
 Good Friday
 Easter Monday
May – Labor Day
 Ascension Day
 Whit Monday
Tuesday after Whit Monday –
 Wäldchestag
18th June – Corpus Christi
3rd October – Day of
 German Unity
18th November – Day of
 Prayer and Repetance
24th December –
 Christmas Eve
25th December – First
 Christmas Day
26th December – Second
 Christmas Day
31st December –
 New Year's Eve

Some shops and offices are open until 2pm on Shrove Tuesday, Wäldchestag, Christmas Eve and New Year's Eve.

Many businesses and restaurants close for vacation (*Urlaub* or *Betriebsferien*) from one to six weeks a year. This may be taken all at once, or part in ski season and part in summer, but unlike Rome or Paris, the entire city does not close down all at once. However, many closings do coincide with school vacations. In Hesse, summer vacation is from mid-June to the end of July, but there are additional lengthy breaks for Christmas and Easter, and shorter ones for Whitsun and autumn break.

No matter what time of year you visit, chances are a festival will be going on. Each village that makes up the city has its traditional celebrations, and there are city-wide events such as the Rose and Light Festival at the Palmengarten in June, and the Christmas Market on the Römerberg in December.

Fireworks are often a part of the festivities, and there are fireworks festivals, such as the Fire and Music shows at the Rebstock in August, in which fireworks are set to music by Tchaikovsky.

On Christmas Eve, between 5 and 5:30 pm, the church bells of the city sound rich, joyful chimes. Crowds gather on the Römerberg to listen to the bells of the St. Paul, St. Leonard and St. Nicholas churches peal, then diminish until one single bell is heard. The best place to listen from is in the middle of the Eiserner Steg above the river.

A variety of sightseeing tours is available to help you to become acquainted with Frankfurt.

## How long to stay

There are numerous cultural and other activities that take place in Frankfurt. Three or four days will be ample time to explore the city. A week will give the tourist a chance to become acquainted with the city and allow time for an excursion or two to the surrounding country. Frankfurt, however, is a more popular attraction for businessmen, who often come for about a

week for conventions or trade fairs that are held in the city.

## How much will it cost?

Thrifty tourists can get by on 70 to 140 DM per day, staying either in the youth hostel or inexpensive hotels.

Travelers with more money to spend will need up to 200 DM per day. Businesspeople should count on at least 500 DM per day if they stay in a top-class hotel. Food, hotel and transport are included in the estimate, but individual living styles are so varied that the cost depends on you. Choice of restaurants and entertainment, and the use of taxis instead of public transport alter the price tag considerably.

Municipal museums charge no entry fee on Sundays (except for special exhibits). On weekdays a nominal fee is charged. Juniors and senior citizens may qualify for lower fees.

## What to wear

Dress for comfort. One sees all manner of clothes, from punk costumes to scruffy jeans to ultra chic. Bring good walking shoes – for women that means low heels and thick soles. For dining out, the theater, or concerts men need suits or sport jackets and women need dresses. Always be prepared for cool weather and rain. Dressing in layers is a good idea.

# PART THREE – PRACTICAL INFORMATION

## Getting into Town

**S-Bahn** train lines S14 and S15 travel between the airport and downtown Frankfurt, running every ten minutes to the main railway station and every 20 minutes to the Hauptwache and Konstablerwache mid-town stations. They run from about 5am to about 8pm, less frequently from 8pm to about midnight, at which time they stop until 4am. Travel time is 10 minutes to the railway station and 15 minutes to downtown.

Line S15 only runs between the airport and the main railway station (on the main railway station level at Track 21; at Track 18 after 8pm). Line S14 is underground at the railway station and downtown stops. It also connects the airport directly with the nearby cities of Mainz and Wiesbaden.

**Bus** 61 connects the airport and the Südbahnhof in Frankfurt-Sachsenhausen, with a travel time of about half an hour. From the Südbahnhof, there are connections to the city underground **U-Bahn** Lines 1, 2 and 3, as well as to trams (*Straßenbahne*n).

### BY AIR
**Airport:** The Rhine-Main Airport is among the most important airports in the world. About 70 airlines and 200 charter companies fly to five continents. Some 20 million passengers pass through Frankfurt each year – an average of 55,000 per day, peaking at as many as 80,000 a day – and the cargo center handles more than a million tons of freight annually.

Nevertheless, it is an easy airport to use, and its baggage handling system is so efficient that it is probably the only major airport in the world that can allow just 45 minutes between connecting flights.

The airport itself has two terminals. Terminal 1 includes three parts, A, B, and C. Areas A and B West are now in the exclusive use of *Lufthansa*, Germany's national airline. Frankfurt is *Lufthansa's* home base.

The newly opened ultramodern Terminal 2 has about a hundred check-in counters and

can handle 12 million passengers a year. The Sky Line, an elevated shuttle train transports travelers between the two terminals. Each train has two cars, one for domestic and one for international flights, so that passengers in transit do not need to leave the passport control and customs area.

Terminal 1 is built on five levels. The railway station is underneath Section B. InterCity express trains stop there on their way to and from Vienna, Klagenfurt, Innsbruck, Amsterdam, Cologne, Dortmund, Hamburg, Hannover, Nürnberg, Regensburg, and Braunschweig.

*Lufthansa* operates an Airport Express train between Düsseldorf, Cologne, Bonn, and Frankfurt Airport four times a day. Passengers holding *Lufthansa* tickets can take this scenic journey along the banks of the Rhine River for the same price as a plane ticket between Frankfurt and any of the three cities. The train stops only at Düsseldorf Airport and at the main railway stations of Düsseldorf, Cologne, and Bonn. Tickets must be purchased before boarding the train. Luggage can be checked through. There is a parking garage which accommodates 10,000 cars.

The third level of the airport is the arrivals area: Section A is for domestic flights and B and C sections for international flights. Information booths can be found in section B. Bank and exchange offices and several restaurants can be found in terminals B and C. Car rental firms have their counters in section A, and travel agencies are in sections A and B. The bus terminal is across the street from section B.

The large Duty Free Shop is in Transit Hall B. There are

*The Hauptbahnhof*

smaller shops in the other transit halls as well. VAT (Value-added-tax) refund claims (see "Important tips for getting around") are processed at customs points at Departure Hall A near gate A13 and before passport control in Departure Hall B. For goods you wish to pack in checked luggage, customs points are at Arrival Hall C near C12 and Arrival Hall B near B6. International Transit Hall B also has a bank and a number of shops.

On the mezzanine above Departure Hall B is the fascinating **Airport Gallery**, which displays rotating art shows and hosts an annual Christmas market. For information, Tel. 6904013 or 6903593

The *Frankfurter Sheraton Hotel*, the largest hotel in Germany, is linked to the terminal by a covered walkway on the mezzanine level between Halls B and C. It has day rates for anyone needing a few hours rest on a long stopover. The nearby *Steigenberger Airport Hotel* has shuttle service on request (see "Accommodation"). Inquire about shuttle service when booking other hotels.

There are no luggage lockers, but left-luggage counters can be found on Arrival Level A and B and on Departure Level between B and C.

The price of airline tickets purchased in Germany is controlled by *Lufthansa* and is

therefore relatively standard. Charters may offer attractive prices, but check for the conditions of use and refunds before you buy. All-inclusive packages for flight and hotel (and sometimes meals and sightseeing) are popular money-savers. Most travel agents will have details.

**BY RAIL**
Frankfurt's *Hauptbahnhof* (abbreviated Hbf) is the busiest passenger station in Germany, handling 1,500 departures and about 260,000 passengers per day.

Europe-wide service includes the fast **EuroCity (EC)** trains, and the slower D trains. Within the country, the **InterCity (IC)** network connects all the major cities hourly during the day. Frankfurt is on three direct IC lines: Frankfurt-Hamburg via the Ruhr Valley, Hamburg-Basel via Hannover and Mannheim, and Dortmund-Munich via Cologne and Würzburg. These trains offer direct connections to cities in Germany and throughout Europe.

Special **ICE** trains pass Frank-

*An unusual entrance to an U-Bahn station*

furt on the route Hamburg-Munich, at hourly intervals. These are fast trains which reach Munich in only 3½ hours (instead of 4 hours and 25 min.) and Hamburg in 3 hours and 40 min. (instead of the usual 6). The ICE trains to Hamburg go via Hannover. Both 1st and 2nd class are available. Reservations – at least one day in advance – are advisable.

The FD and D trains are also express trains but are not as fast or as modern.

A fast-train surcharge (*Zuschlag*) is usually collected for EC and IC trains, and it is slightly less expensive when purchased with the ticket or from an automat in the station than on board the train.

Sleeper trains for long-distance travel have first- and second-class compartments and inexpensive couchettes. Some night trains have regular seating compartments that usually do not require reservations.

A diagram of the makeup of the express trains is posted trackside (look for the board that says *Wagenstandanzeigen*), so if you have a reservation you know exactly where your car will stop. Automatic boards at each track announce the departures.

Cars can be transported on trains from the loading point at the nearby town of Neu Isenberg which is south of Frankfurt. These trains usually serve ski resorts in winter and beach resorts in summer.

Local and regional train lines extend from the Hauptbahnhof as well as from smaller stations. The Südbahnhof in Sachsenhausen has lines to Wächtersbach, Bad Soden-Salmünster, Gelnhausen, Hanau, Anschaffenburg, and Miltenberg; the Ostbahnhof to Hanau and Anschaffenburg (as well as buses to Dörnigheim and Hanau); and the Frankfurt-Höchst to Königstein, Wiesbaden, and Niedernhausen (and buses to Königstein and Bad Soden). The E trains run moderately fast regional service, and N trains follow the milk runs.

The *Europabus* Touring

terminal is at the southern side of the railway station (Südausgang). The ticket office is located in the railway station, but can only be reached from the street, at 4 Mannheimer Straße. Bus connections are posted in the station, although not as prominently or frequently as the train schedules.

Arrival (white) and Departure (yellow) schedules are posted throughout the station. The schedule to the airport is posted separately on white paper headed by an airport logo. The trains are listed by arrival or departure time (and German trains usually run on time), using the 24-hour clock. The schedule gives the destination and major stops en route, the type of train, whether a dining car is attached, and the days when the train does not run.

Germany is one of the countries that accepts *Eurailpass* for unlimited train travel. The pass must be purchased outside Europe and is available for 15 or 21 days, or one, two or three months. It is valid for first-class travel without fast-train surcharges and for passage or discounts on many ferries, river boats, lake steamers, and buses. A second-class *Eurail Youth Pass* is available for people under 26 years of age, for one or two months. A *Saver Pass* for two or three persons traveling together is available for 15 days.

For those who plan to travel by rail within Germany only, the *Deutsche Bundesbahn* (DB), the German Federal Railway, offers a German Rail Pass. It is good for unlimited travel for four, nine or sixteen days in first- or second-class. The *Junior Pass* is available for nine or sixteen days. Another youth-fare ticket is the *Tramper One-Month Ticket* for those under age 23, and students under age 27.

Beneath the station are the regional S-Bahn train tracks and a three-level parking garage. A tram stop in front of the station can be reached through an underground passage.

Inside the station, on track level, there are restaurants and snack bars, food shops, newsstands and book stores. Above the Buffet Vitesse (across from Track 3), a self-service restaurant is open 6am-11pm. The food is reasonable, and prices are moderate. Choose a table overlooking either the tracks or the city.

The bank and exchange office is past Track 1 (*Südausgang*) and is open 6:30am-10pm. A *Geldautomat* across from Track 15 changes certain foreign currencies. The machine also has an automatic teller for holders of *EuroCard*.

**The Tourist Information Hauptbahnhof Office** opposite Track 23 books hotel rooms, organizes sightseeing, and dispenses information about the city. (Open Mon.-

Sat., April-October, 8am-10pm, from November-March, 8am-9pm, Sun. and holidays 9:30am-8pm.)

The *Reisezentrum* (travel information office), at the corner of the main corridor across from Tracks 12/13, provides train schedules, reserves seats or sleepers, handles Rail/Drive car rentals and sells rail tickets for outside Germany. It is open 6am-10:45pm. Ticket windows for inland travel are in the main corridor. Tickets for the Frankfurt area, within a 50 kilometer radius but outside the city transport system, are sold only in the red automats.

The track level of the station also has a *DER* Reisebüro (travel agency) at Airport Arrival Hall B that offers complete services. Open daily 8am-9pm.

Coin operated luggage lockers have instructions in English and can be used for up to 72 hours. Money is deposited for the first 24 hours of usage. Charges for the remaining time used is payed when luggage is retrieved. Luggage left longer than 72 hours in a locker will be removed and taken to the *Reisegepäck* (left-luggage) counter behind Track 14, which is open around the clock. Bags can also be checked there if you wish to have them sent on the train (Tel. 2655834).

A Trade Fair Information booth stands near Track 11, and a Train Information booth near Tracks 12/13.

A small art gallery across from Tracks 4/5 displays periodic exhibitions. *Art in Bahnhof* posters announce the shows. During an exhibition period the gallery is open daily 10am-6pm, and entry is free.

Upstairs is a post and telephone office, open 24 hours a day (parcel service is not available at night). A three-screen movie theater above the *Reisezentrum* shows mainly X-rated films.

The lost and found office outside the *Südausgang* is open from 1:30am-4pm. There is a *Bahnhofs Mission* (social service facility) across from the exchange office.

## In-town Transportation

**Public Transportation**: The Frankfurt transportation authority (*FVV*) operates a superb network of buses, *Straßenbahnen* (trams), underground trains (*U-Bahn*) and regional commuter trains (*S-Bahn*). Bus and tram stops are marked by a green H on a yellow circle. U-Bahn entrances are marked by a white U on a blue square. S-Bahn entrances are marked by a white S on a green circle.

A uniform tariff applies to all

forms of city public transportation, based on distance and including transfers. No tickets are sold on board trains or trams, and the fine for riding without a ticket is stiff. It is collected on-the-spot by plain clothed individuals who sometimes check for *Schwarzfahrer* (riders without tickets).

Tickets can be purchased in the blue automats at each stop or from bus drivers at stops that have no machines. English instructions are posted on the automats.

A color-coded map on the machine shows the destinations. The city center is Zone 1 (yellow); the airport is in Zone 2 (green); farther afield are Zones 3 (red) and 4 (blue). Note that the fare is higher during rush hours, 6:30-8:30am and 4-6:30pm.

The machines give change along with the ticket unless the words *Bitte abgezählt zahlen* (use correct change) appear. If you do not have the correct change but wish to

*An U-Bahn sign*

*An S-Bahn sign*

buy a ticket anyway, push the white button beside the notice, *Nur bei Verzicht auf Restgeld Taste drücken*, which indicates that you will get a ticket but forfeit your change. If the words *außer Betrieb* appear, the machine is out of order.

During the day public transport runs as often as every three minutes, but is limited between about midnight and 6am.

Maps of the transportation system are available at *FVV* offices, Tourist Information Offices and some book shops and newsstands.

Using U-Bahn and S-Bahn facilities is not recommended if you are alone at night. They are not safe, since groups of youngsters and junkies may hold up travelers on trains and in the downtown stations.

**Taxis**: A fleet of radio-equipped taxis works 24 hours a day with the same rates under telephone 250001, 230001 or 230033. The price on the meter is the price you pay, regardless of the number of passengers or amount of baggage. All major credit cards are accepted. You may request a credit-card taxi when you order one. It is not uncommon to round off the fare to the next mark or so as a tip. If you need a receipt, ask for a *Quittung*.

Taxi stands are located throughout the city, especially at the airport and the main railway station. To hail a taxi, step to the curb and raise your hand; a lighted rooftop sign indicates the taxi is free.

### CAR RENTAL

Frankfurt has a number of car rental agencies, many offering weekend rates from Friday at noon until Monday at 9am with unlimited mileage. Some have offices at the airport in Arrival Hall A, as well as offices in town, with hotel pick-up and delivery.

Here is a list of some car rental agencies:

*Avis*: Airport Arrival Hall A, Tel. 69027771; Main Station, Tel. 234254.

*Europcar*: Airport Arrival Hall A, Tel. 6905464; Main Station, Tel. 244002.

Hertz: Airport Arrival Hall A, Tel. 69050111; Main station, Tel. 240484; Toll Free Reservations, Tel. 0130-2121.

*Alamo Rent A Car*: Frankfurt Airport – Frankfurt Downtown, Tel. (toll free) 0130-846424.

*Turtle Rent*: 34 Gerbermühl-straße, Tel. 621105.

*Limousine travel Service*: 39 Wiesenhüttenplatz, Tel. 230492.

Rented cars are readily available in all price ranges. Visitors may want to use Fly/Drive or Rail/Drive packages available through travel agents, the airlines, or the DB.

### DRIVING IN FRANKFURT

Traffic flow within the city is facilitated by the City Ring, a road that follows the crescent of the old city wall. Directions are well marked, but numerous one-way streets (*Einbahn-straße*n) complicate matters. The driver accustomed to a grid pattern of city blocks may become hopelessly entangled in the winding streets whose names change frequently for no apparent reason, as is the custom in Europe. Finding an exact address is complicated by the fact that numbers are missing from many buildings. The street names posted at intersections, however, show the building numbers within the block.

Drivers would be well advised to purchase a map that indicates one-way streets, building numbers, and parking garages. A map of the city center (*Stadtmitte*) is available in some book shops, newsstands, and stationery stores. Ask for the *Falk Touristplan*.

Street side parking is all but impossible in the downtown area during business hours and the police are conscientious about issuing tickets. No-parking areas are indicated by a circle with a red X against a blue background, and restricted parking is indicated by the same circle with a red diagonal slash.

Some intersections have no stop or yield signs; at such junctions the car on the right has the right of way. Watch out for bicycle traffic. Where there are no bike paths, cyclists use the streets. When driving be extremely careful at zebra crossings – cars MUST stop when a pedestrian starts to cross.

Traffic usually flows smoothly on the *Autobahn*, slowing at rush hour, and may come to a halt during vacation periods.

As a rule, there are no speed limits on the *Autobahn* – though limits are posted at some busy intersections in Frankfurt – and cars drive as fast as 220 kilometers per hour (about 140 mph). For safety's sake, and to avoid getting a heavy fine, use the left lane only to pass. Double-check the rearview mirror before making a lane change as cars can appear on your bumper in the blink of an eye.

German police do not stop cars for speeding or passing red lights. Automatic cameras photograph speeding cars at radar checkpoints and at stop lights and the drivers get a ticket three to six months later.

On the *Autobahn*, yellow emergency phones are set up every kilometer. Arrows on the black-and-white signposts indicate in the direction of the nearest phone. The German automobile club ADAC has a breakdown service (Tel. 19211). Reciprocal benefits are available to members of auto clubs in other countries.

## Accommodation

Frankfurt has excellent hotels in the luxury range, as well as cozy, inexpensive *Pensionen* and a youth hostel on the banks of the Main River.

Breakfast (*Frühstück*) may be included in the price of a room and typically consists of coffee or tea, rolls or sliced whole-grain bread, honey or marmalade, and often an egg. Sometimes cold cuts and spreadable wursts are included. Some of the larger and more luxurious hotels have breakfast buffets.

Many hotels have rooms without private baths or toilets. Request a *Zimmer mit Dusche* (shower) or *Bad* (bath) and *Toilette* (toilet). It is a good idea to have a look at rooms at the less-expensive hotels before you decide to stay. Tax is included in the price.

A great many hotels, including some of the best, are found in the vicinity of the main railway station. There is one hotel directly connected to the airport and two others nearby.

If you arrive in Frankfurt without hotel reservations, booking services are available in the airport at DER Reise-büro, Arrival Hall B, open daily 8am-9pm and at Flughafen Frankfurt/Main AG-Travel Agency, Arrival Hall B5, open daily 8am-9pm. At the main railway station, the Tourist Information Office opposite Track 23 can book rooms for you. Tel. 212-38849/51 (Open Mon.-Sat. 8am-10pm from April-October, and 8am-9pm Nov.-March. Open 9:30am-8pm on Sundays and holidays year round.)

The following hotels have been classified into the categories listed below, based on two-persons occupancy (double room):

A – from 360 DM
B – from 230 DM
C – from 190 DM
D – from 100 DM

### AT THE AIRPORT
*Frankfurt Sheraton Hotel*: (A) directly connected to the airport. Tel. 69770; fax 69772230. Plush with indoor swimming pool, sauna and restaurant.

*Steigenberger Frankfurt Airport*: (A) 16 Untersch weinstiege. Tel. 69750; fax 69752505. Convenient access to airport. Rooms are a bit plain, but equipped with an indoor swimming pool, sauna, and restaurant.

## NEAR THE HAUPTBAHNHOF

*Hotel National*: (B) 50 Baselerstraße. Tel. 27394-0; fax. 234460. Includes a bar and offers special allowances and facilities for children.

*Frankfurt Intercontinental*: (A) 43 Wilhelm-Leuschner-Straße. Tel. 26050; fax. 252467. Popular with international business travelers, with all the comforts to which they are accustomed.

*Mövenpick Parkhotel Frankfurt*: (A) 28-38 Wiesenhüttenplatz. Tel. 26970; fax. 2697884. "The Little Grand Hotel" prides itself on luxurious service and surroundings. The Casablanca piano bar is a good place to relax.

*Pullman Hotel Savigny*: (B) 14-16 Savignystraße. Tel. 75330; fax. 7533175. A good hotel on an elegant street.

## THE CITY CENTER

*Schwille*: (B) 50 Große Bockenheimer Straße (in the Freßgass'). Tel. 92010-0; fax. 92010-999. You cannot get any closer to the center of activity. A good café downstairs.

*Weißes Haus*: (D) 18 Jahnstraße. Tel. 9591180, fax 5963912. In a residential area, but within walking distance of the main shopping area. Reasonable restaurant.

*Uebe*: (D), 3 Grüneburgweg. Tel. 591209. Simple but comfortable. Located between the Opera and the Palmengarten.

*Steigenberger Frankfurter Hof*: (A) 17 Kaiserplatz. Tel. 21502; fax. 215900. One of the city's

best hotels, with one of the best restaurants.

*Turm-Hotel*: (C) 20 Escher-sheimer Landstraße. Tel. 154050, fax 553578. Comfortable. A good location for theater crowd.

### NEAR THE MESSE
*Hessischer Hof*: (A) 40 Friedrich-Ebert-Anlage. Tel. 75400; fax. 7540924. Between the Fairgrounds and the main railway station. Owned by brother-Princes of Hessen. Superb interior, good food.

*Palmenhof*: (B) 89-91 Bocken-heimer Landstraße. Tel. 7530060, fax 75300-666. On a busy street, near the Palmen-garten.

*Ramada Hotel Frankfurt*: (A) 180 Oeserstraße. Tel. 39050; fax 3808218. Providing the comfort one expects from this chain.

### SACHSENHAUSEN
*Holiday Inn Frankfurt*: (A) 1 Mailänderstraße. Tel. 68020; fax. 6802333. Away from the center of town, but a good view of the city from the upper floors.

*Hotel Primus*: (C) 19 Große Rittergasse. Tel. 623020; fax 621238. A place for people who prefer a quiet surroundings.

*Hotel Hübler*: (C) 91-93 Große Rittergasse. Tel. 616038, 613132. Close to the nightlife. Simple rooms.

### YOUTH HOSTEL
*Haus der Jugend*: 12 Deutschherrnufer. Tel. 619058. For anyone on a tight budget. Directly on the Main. Youth cards, required for admittance, can be purchased here. Young people are given preference.

### OUTLYING AREAS
*Burghof Hotel*: (D) Anne Krämer, 6 Am Weiher, Dreieich. Tel. 06103-84002, fax 88819.

*Novotel Frankfurt/Eschborn*: (B) 10 Philipp-Helfmann-Straße. Tel. 06196-9010. Standard, satisfactory rooms.

## Hotels out of town
During the larger trade fairs it may be impossible to find a room in Frankfurt. The excellent transportation system makes it practical to stay in a neighboring town or city. If you stay in villages around Taunus, however, you may require a car.

### OFFENBACH
*Hotel Kaiserhof*: (D) 8a Kaiserstraße. Tel. 814054, fax 816430. A few steps from the railway station. Excellent Russian restau rant.

### NEU-ISENBURG

*Gravenbruch-Kempinski-Frankfurt:* (A) Gravenbruch. Tel. 06102-5050, fax 505445. Luxurious rooms, gourmet restaurant.

*Isabella-Hotel Frankfurt*: (B) 61-63 Herzogstraße. Tel. 06102-3570, fax 357211. Very comfortable.

### KRONBERG

*Schloßhotel*: (A) 25 Hainerstraße. Tel. 06173-7011. The original "Guest in a Castle" hotel. A great place to get away from the crowds.

### MAINZ

*Hilton Hotel*: (A) 68 Rheinstraße. Tel. 06131-2450. On the Rhine River. Convenient if you are interested in easy access to the cruise ships.

### WIESBADEN

*Nassauer Hof*: (A) 3 Kaiser-Friedrich-Platz. Tel. 0611-1330, fax 133632. Luxury hotel across the street from the casino. One of Germany's best restaurants is housed in the hotel.

*Best Western Penta Hotel*: (B) 15 Auguste-Viktoria-Straße. Tel. 0611-33060, fax 303960. Pleasant, standard accommodations.

*Admiral Hotel*: (C) 8 Geisbergstraße. Tel. 0611-58660, fax 521053.

### DARMSTADT

*Maritim Konferenzhotel Hotel*: (B) 105 Rheinstraße. Tel. 06151-15880, fax 1588800. Comfortable, and near the railway station with good access to Frankfurt via the *autobahn*.

*Weinmichel*: (C) 10 Schleiermacherstraße. Tel. 06151-26822. Rooms small but comfortable. Good restaurant.

## Practical Tips

## Business hours

Shops open Mon.-Fri. 9am-6pm; Thur. 9am-8:30pm. Bakeries and news agents may open as early as 6:30am. Smaller shops may close for lunch for an hour or more between noon and 3pm.

Most Saturdays, shops must close at 2pm, while some close earlier or do not reopen. The first Saturday of the month and every Saturday in Advent are *Langer Samstag* (Long Saturday), April-September 9am-4pm, October-March 9am-6pm. Difference in business hours of some stores are possible.

Shops open late at the airport only allow purchases to be made by persons holding airline tickets. The central railway station has also longer store hours.

Many **offices** close as early as

2pm on Friday and remain closed on Saturday. Some offices open as early as 7:30am. If you need information from a business office, the best time to call is between 9am and noon, or 2:30 and 4pm.

### BANKS

Banks are usually open Mon.-Fri. 8am-12:30pm and 1:30-4pm. They may close early Friday but stay open until 6pm on Thursday. After-hours exchange offices operate at the airport and main railway station.

### PHARMACIES

Pharmacies take turns providing night and weekend service. The name and address of the on-duty pharmacy in the area is posted in each pharmacy's window.

## Postal service and telephones

It is hard to miss the bright yellow signs of the *Bundespost* (German Post Office). Post offices are open 8am-6pm Mon.-Fri., until noon Saturday.

The main post office is in the center of town, at 108 Zeil. It has an after-hours counter open Mon.-Sat. until 9pm, and on Sat. 8am-6pm, Sun. 12am-4pm. Services include telex, telefax and general delivery.

The post office at the main railway station is open 24 hours a day, but package service is not available between 6pm-8am. Telegram service is also available.

The post office at the airport in Departures Level Waiting Area B is open daily 6am-10pm; in Departures Level Transit Area B Mon.-Sat. 7am-9pm, Sun and holidays 8am-4:30pm; in the east of the Terminal C, Mon.-Fri. 8am-1pm, 2pm-6pm, Sat. 8-12pm.

In writing an address, the Frankfurt postal code 6000 is placed before the name of the city, along with a D for *Deutschland* (Germany). The district code comes after the city: D-6000 Frankfurt a.M. 1, for example.

Post offices provide a number of services, including payment of bills, a savings bank, and foreign currency exchange facilities at the larger offices. Some terms you may need to help you read the signs posted over the service windows include: *Briefmarken* (stamps), *Paket* (Packages), *Päckchen* (small packages), *Einschreiben* (registered letters).

You may want to send your

letters per *Eilboten* (express) or *Luftpost* (air mail), and when you mail a package out of the country, you will have to fill out a *Zoll* (customs) form. Incidentally, the post office sells packing kits in several sizes, including the box, tape, string and address forms.

Outdoor mailboxes are also bright yellow. Some may have two slots, *Frankfurt* (local mail) and *Andere Orte* (for letters going outside the city). Collection times are posted on each box.

### TELEPHONES

Telephoning from a hotel can be extremely expensive, especially for calls to the United States or Australia, because the hotel adds a surcharge. Before making a long-distance call, find out how much this surcharge is. It may be worth your while to call from the post office.

Post offices are equipped with private telephone cabins. Go to the telephone window and you will be assigned a booth where you can dial your number. The clerk can tell you the country or city code if you do not know it. A set of phone books for the entire country is usually available, too. When you have finished your call, return to the window and pay for the call. It is much more convenient than trying to feed coins into a phone for a lengthy long-distance call, and you get a receipt for business purposes.

*Outside the Central Post Office*

Most phones accept phone cards for a fixed number of call units. They can be purchased at post offices at the main railway station, at Hall B of the airport and on the Zeil.

Direct dial is available from Germany to over 180 countries and territories worldwide.

**The Frankfurt city phone code** is **069** when dialing from within Germany and **69** when dialing from most other countries. It is not needed within the city.

Some phone booths have emergency call switches that require no money. These booths are marked in red with *SOS Notrufmelder*.

## Currency and exchange

Most banks and the larger post offices have *Wechsel* (change) counters. Rates at commercial change offices (which keep longer hours than banks) may be higher than bank rates. Some restaurants and shops popular with the U.S. military, of which there are many,

accept U.S. dollars, usually at usurious rates.

Bank rates may slightly vary, but seldom enough to make it worthwhile to spend time shopping around, unless you plan to change a large amount of money. Daily rates are usually posted in the window.

## Tourist services

The Verkehrsamt Tourist Board is located at 52 Kaiserstraße, Tel. 212-38800.

The Frankfurt Tourist Information Office is located at Central Railway Station, opposite Track 23, Tel. 21238849/51. (Open April-October, weekdays 8am-10pm, November-March weekdays 8am-9pm, Sun. and holidays year round 9:30am-8pm.)

There is also a branch at 27 Römerberg. Tourist Information Römer, Tel. 21238708/9. (Open daily 9am-6pm.)

## Services for business visitors

The following is a list of spe-cialized services that might be useful to business visitors in Frankfurt. Check the yellow pages (*Gelbe Seiten*) for telephone numbers and addresses.

*Büro Service*: For office services, including long or short-term office rental, telex, telefax, multilingual secretaries, post and telephone answering services.

*Übersetzer*: Translators.
*Dolmetscher:* Interpreters.
*Kurierdienste:* Courier service.
*Detektive:* Armed transport and personal guards.
*Druckereien:* Printing.
*Film:* Film studios.
*Fotografen:* Photographers.

## Tipping

There are no hard and fast rules about tipping in Germany. Service charges are often included on bills, but it is customery to add some 10% more (in restaurants when the menu notes *MWT & Bedienung Inklusiv*, it means that tax and service are included). In hotels, tip the concierge according to service, give the bellman 1-2DM per bag and the chambermaid 1-2DM per day.

Give gas station attendants 1-2DM for extra service, hairdressers 10 to 15 percent, with something extra for the person who washed your hair, and taxi drivers about 5 percent (rounding to an even DM makes it easy).

## Drinking

The drinking age in Germany is 16 years for beer and wine, and 18 years for hard liquor. Hours that liquor can be sold is determined by the kind of license the restaurant or bar has. Many Germans drink a *Schnaps* or *Digestif* (both strong alcoholic drinks) with their mid-morning "second breakfast."

Beer and wine are popular. Wine bars may have one or two kinds of beer and pubs that specialize in a wide range of beers will probably have a few types of wine.

The most popular Frankfurt drink is *Apfelwein* (apple wine). (See "Wining and Dining" for a detailed listing of apple wine bars.)

## VAT refunds

There are heavy taxes on goods and services in Germany. The *Mehrwertsteuer* (MWT), the VAT (valued-added tax), is 14 percent. With a little time and effort visitors can get a tax rebate of about 12 percent on purchases.

Ask the shop clerk if their stores participates in the rebate plan. Some shops advertise tax free plans. Others do not post "tax free" signs, but offer the service. After presenting your passport to the shopkeeper, you will receive a green form that must be filled out. Present the form and the unused items at a customs station when you leave the country. The customs official will stamp the form. Send the form back to the shop and a refund in DM will be mailed to you. It is possible to collect refunds at the bank inside Transit Hall B at the airport or at branches of the Deutsche Verkehrs- und Kreditbank. Refunds cannot be credited to credit cards.

## A matter of manners

Knowing how customs in Germany differ from those at home can prevent you from making an embarassing *faux pas* during your visit.

Politeness is the rule for business and social occasions. Make appointments instead of just dropping in – even if you must telephone ahead on very short notice. Avoid making business appointments for Friday afternoon as many offices close early. If you include lunch in your business affairs, discuss business before or after, but not during the meal.

Note that a person answers the phone by giving his last name instead of saying hello. The German word *morgen* can

mean morning and also tomorrow. Use *morgen früh* (literally "early morning") if you wish to make an appointment for the following day.

Adults do not use first names unless they are invited to. Do not invite your counterpart to do so if he or she is older than yourself. This is a gesture that must be initiated by the elder of the two.

The Germans are sticklers for titles. Women over 20 are *Frau*, whether or not they are married. Always use a person's full title: *Herr Professor*, *Frau Dr.*, even *Herr Dr.*

Anything goes with dress in Frankfurt, but for businesspersons conservative attire is advisable. For theater and parties, men should wear dark suits and ties, and women wear dresses.

At dinner or cocktail hour, wait until everyone has a glass and a toast is made before you take a sip. The toast to good health is usually just *Zum Wohl* or *Prosit* – the first being the

more formal. However, at restaurants food is often brought as it is ready, so it is alright to begin eating before everyone at the table is served. Wish your companions *Guten Appetit* before they begin.

## Measurements, electricity, and time

**Measurements**: Germany uses the metric system. The following tables will help you make conversions.

Weight: 28.35 grams – 1 ounce
453 grams – 1 pound
1 kilogram – 2.2 pounds

Capacity: 0.47 liters – 1 pint
1 liter – approximately 1 quart
3.79 liters – 1 gallon

Distance: 2.54 centimeters – 1 inch
30.5 centimeters – 1 foot
1 meter – approximately 39 inches
1 kilometer – 0.628 miles
1.609 kilometers – 1 mile

The most difficult conversion to negotiate is from Celsius to Fahrenheit. Multiply by 9/5 (nine-fifths) and add 32.

**Electrical Current** in Germany is 220 volts. Some hotels also have 110-volt razor plugs. Sockets are usually round and recessed. Visitors from Great Britain will need plug adapters for their 220-volt appliances. Americans will need both adapters (to fit the socket) and converters (to change the voltage).

All-purpose converters and adapters that can be changed to fit most sockets are available at luggage and travel shops. Hotels may be able to provide converters and adapters as well. If you have dual-voltage appliances, remember to set them to the proper voltage – otherwise you may blow a fuse or melt your appliance.

**Time** in Frankfurt is GMT (Greenwich Mean Time) +1 and is six hours ahead of New York (Eastern Standard Time). It changes to European Summer Time (daylight savings time) the last Sunday in March and back again to Eastern Standard time the last Sunday in September.

**FRANKFURT**

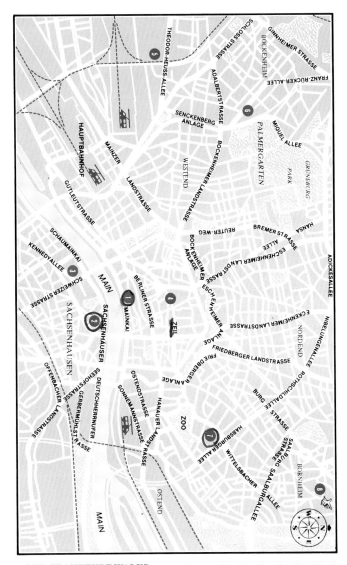

## OUR FRANKFURT WALKS

# GETTING TO KNOW THE CITY

There is always something happening in Frankfurt; be it at the Stock Exchange or the Opera. Even on Saturday afternoon, the quietest time in Germany, Frankfurters are out and about.

*The Main waterfront*

## CITY BUS TOURS

Frankfurt's Tourist Board offers many opportunities to explore the city from many different angles, be it on a tour of the most outstanding attractions of Frankfurt am Main or on a special tour with selected highlights.

The Tourist Board offers in Summer morning bus tours from March 1 to October 31, daily at 10.30am, including the visit of Goethehaus. In Winter the tour includes the visit to Europaturm. From Nov. 1 to Feb. 28, daily at 10am; 10.30am or 11.45am. The Afternoon Bus Tours are daily in March, April, October and from May to September Monday to Saturday, departure at 2pm.

The Taunus Mountain Tours are from May 2 to September 30, includes visits to the Hessenpark and the old town of Höchst, departure time each Sunday at 2pm. Tel. 212-38800 for reservations.

### CITY TRAM TOURS

*The Ebbelwei Express* – Applewine Express – is a brightly-painted vintage tram which makes trips through Sachsenhausen and downtown on weekends and holidays between about 1:30-5:30pm. Trains leave every 40 minutes. You can begin or end the ride at any stop.

The fare (buy the ticket on board) includes one glass of apple wine or apple juice and a bag of pretzels. The *Ebbelwei Express* can be rented for group parties. Contact *Stadtwerke Frankfurt a.M*, Tel. 213-22425 for more information.

### STEAM TRAIN TOUR

On some Saturdays and Sundays, an old steam train chugs along the banks of the Main River from the Eiserner Steg west to Frankfurt-Griesheim or east to Frankfurt-Mainkur and back. There are no stops, but there is a buffet car. Saturday trips are hourly from 1-5pm, Sunday trips hourly from 10am-noon and 2-5pm. For information, contact *Historische Eisenbahn Frankfurt e.V.*, Tel. 436093.

*An excursion boat waiting for passengers*

### BOAT TRIPS

Boat Trips on the Main River are primarily operated by two firms, each of which have landing stages at the Eiserner Steg.

*Fahrgastschiffahrt Wikinger II* provides boat trips between Gerbermühle and Griesheim from about Easter to mid-September, weekdays at 2pm, 3pm, and 4pm and Sundays and holidays every half hour beginning at 1pm. If weather permits, there are weekday cruises at 5pm and Sunday cruises at 11am. Tel. 282886 or 293960 for more information.

*Frankfurter Personenschiffahrt* runs a similar cruise between Gerbermühle and Schwanheim/Goldstein during the same season. Weather permitting, trips leave daily at 2pm, 3pm, 4pm, and 5pm. Addition trips on Sunday leave at 11am, noon, and 1pm. At intervals during June, July, and August, the firm also has trips to Rüdesheim and Assmannshausen on the Rhine, to

Seligenstadt and Aschaffenburg on the Main, and to Klingenberg (famous for its red wine) on the Main. Tel. 281884 or 282884 for additional information.

Both companies offer charter trips year round for groups of 50 or more.

On the cruises aboard the *Wikinger II* or *Vaterland*, you can choose only one direction or make the full round trip. If you choose the latter (it lasts about two hours), stay on board when the boat docks at the Eiserner Steg before heading in the opposite direction.

The ships pass the "office city" of highrises in Niederrad, the pastel-painted waterworks building, an in-city campground and a small yacht harbor to the west. On the eastward half of the journey there is a detour through the Frankfurt harbor (built in the 1930s), the huge automobile graveyard and the Molenkopf, base of operations for the river's fireboats.

### AIRPORT TOURS

Those who are interested in the technical composition of an airport can receive a guided tour of the *Rhine-Main* Airport's service, maintenance, and other facilities. Tours are lead on request in German, English, and French. Contact Tel. 69070291 for information and reservations.

### BIRD'S EYE VIEW

Flights in small airplanes and helicopters, departing from Frankfurt Airport, fly over the city and the region. For such fine bird's eye view contact *Classic Wings*, Tel. 550265.

### INDIVIDUAL GUIDES

A group of friendly Frankfurters got together in 1980 to find a way to introduce visitors to the best that the city has to offer. Today, members of the Freundeskreis Liebenswertes Frankfurt e.V. (Circle of Friends), Tel. 479361, a non-profit organization, will take you for a stroll "behind the scenes." Leave a message and someone will return your call. For an English-speaking person, Tel. 583922 or 594156 after 6pm. These informal guides can also be conducted in French, Spanish, or Japanese.

Guests who book flights through or to Frankfurt on *Lufthansa* or other IATA-member airlines, are entitled to a coupon good for free or reduced-rate activities in the city. They include city sightseeing tours, museum entries, zoo and Palmengarten visits, use of the casino buses, theater performances, and excursions outside the city. To redeem the coupon, see the Airport

Travel Agency, Arrival Hall B5 or the Tourist Information Office in the main railway station or at the Hauptwache (TK).

You can have a sightseeing tour of Frankfurt by taxi. This service is provided in several languages, and takes some 2-3 hours. Contact *Taxi Union Frankfurt*, Tel. 230033/230001.

# FRANKFURT – AREA BY AREA

The best way to get to know Frankfurt is to walk through each *Viertel* (quarter). The streets of Frankfurt are seldom on a square-grid pattern: the tangled maze of streets is typical of European cities that expanded in a haphazard way long before wide thoroughfares were needed. One-way streets, a problem for drivers, will hardly concern you. However, finding street names can be frustrating; the small blue signs are usually posted at only one corner of an intersection.

Be careful not to confuse three main streets: Eschenheimer Landstraße, Eckenheimer Straße, and Eschenheimer Anlage.

*Frankfurt on the Main*

## The Römerberg – Where It All Began

The gently-sloping Römerberg, though it can hardly be called a hill, stood high enough to offer early settlers protection from the flooding of the Main River. The river brought trade, and since its early days, despite its Imperial status, Frankfurt was a city of merchants. Even the Römer, the town hall, was originally a conglomeration of merchants' houses.

You can reach the Römerberg by U-Bahn Line 4 or Straßenbahn 11. Drivers can find an underground garage (Parkhaus Römer) next to the Cathedral.

Begin the tour by passing the **Historical Garden** (Historischer Garten) and the **Schirn Art Hall** (Schirn Kunsthalle), a juxtaposition of old and new. (Remember that most museums close on Monday.) The car park and U-Bahn exits are right next to the Historical Garden. The archeological excavations of the Garden have brought to light Roman and Carolingian remains.

*The dome of the post-modern Schirn Art Hall*

The post modern Schirn Art Hall (an old Frankfurt word for the open-front shops of the old town) is the venue for exhibitions, concerts and plays, and has a glass enclosed coffee house on the ground floor. Many Frankfurters object to its blocking the view of the nearby Cathedral and to the arrangement of the exhibition space inside. Open Tues.-Fri. 10am-9pm, Sat. and Sun. 10am-7pm.

Behind the Historical Garden is the **Dom** or **St. Bartholomew's Cathedral** (Open daily 9-6pm, in winter until 5pm, closed Mon 12:30-3pm. Guided tours Tues.-Fri. at 3pm. Tel. 290787.) Built of local red sandstone on the site of the ninth-century Salvator church, it was rededicated in 1238. It has held Cathedral status since 1356, and in 1562 it became the

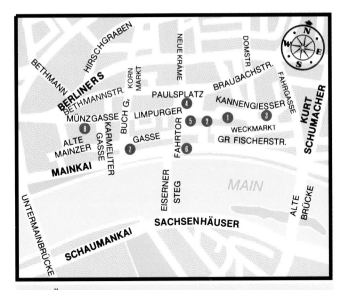

### THE RÖMERBERG

1. Historischer Garten
2. Schirn Art Gallery
3. Dom Cathedral
4. Römerberg
5. Alte Nikolaikirche
6. Historisches Museum
7. Leonhardskirche
8. Karmeliterkloster

*Kaiserdom* (Imperial Cathedral), the coronation place for the emperors of the Holy Roman Empire of the German Nation.

Its huge Gothic tower and spire are city landmarks. Two Carolingian towers originally adorned the Cathedral, but were demolished after it was determined that they appeared out of proportion to the Gothic Cathedral. Construction of the tower that you see today began in 1415 and was completed in 1877. After the devastation of World War II, the tower remained standing above the rubble. There is a fee to climb the 383 winding steps; only worthwhile on clear days when there is a marvelous view. (Open daily 9am-12:30pm and 2:30-6pm.)

Before visiting the actual Cathedral, look into the **Dom Museum** at the main entrance. (Open Tues.-Fri. 10am-5pm, Sat. and Sun.

11am-5pm. Guided tours Tues.-Fri. at 11am.)

The interior of the Cathedral is lofty and at first glance gives the impression of having little adornment. However, its Gothic altars merit a close look. Most of them were collected from all over Germany by the parish priest Münzenberger. On the west wall are epitaphs of the Thurn and Taxis family. Coats of arms of the patrician families of Frankfurt – Glauburg, Holzhausen, Weiß von Limpurg, and Monis – are on the back wall of the nave.

From the Cathedral, you can reach the Römerberg by either walking along the Saalgasse or past the Technical Town Hall, passing a small arcade of shops. The *Vieille Provence* there sells products from the south of France, including very lovely scented soaps.

If you want brochures or information about the city, stop at the **Presse-und Informationsamt**; it is well-marked. This is not a tourist office, but it provides historical information. (Open daily 8:30am-4:30pm, Sat. until noon.)

The **Römerberg**, an elongated five-sided square, was the site of the first trade fairs in the city. The area was left as a large open space, free of buildings, to accommodate royal parades and ceremonies. The square soon developed into the center of public life in Frankfurt. The **Fountain of Justice** (Gerechtigkeitsbrunnen), approximately in the center, was erected between 1541 and 1543, while the figure of Justice was not added until 1610. During the coronation of the Emperor Matthias in 1614 wine was dispensed from special fittings in the shape of

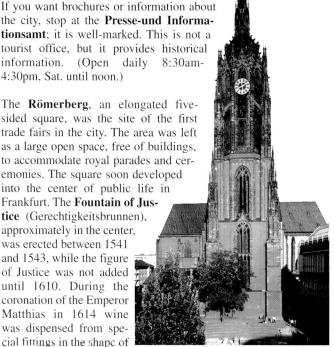

*The Dom, with its huge Gothic tower and spire, is a city landmark*

*The lofty interior of the Dom*

an eagle's and a lion's head. This extravagance has not been repeated, but during festivals wine is served from stands around the fountain.

In 1887, a wine dealer, G.D. Manskopf, had the worn original stone figures of Justice (without a blindfold), the Sirens, and the reliefs of the Virtues copied and cast in bronze. The wrought-iron railings were also added at that time.

An allegorical figure of Justice faces the five-gabled facade of the **Röme**r (the historic old Town Hall). In the early days, the town hall stood where the Cathedral tower now stands, but it was damaged by fire and was subsequently deemed too small for the elaborate Imperial ceremonies. In 1405, the Council of Magistrates purchased the Römer and the Golden Swan (Goldener Schwan). Over the next 400 years, the town hall expanded, incorporating another nine houses.

Today the complex is used for the annual Christmas fair, the Main festival, and various cultural and political events.

*The Fountain of Justice*

The square was almost completely devastated in World War II, and most of what you see today has been reconstructed. As you face the Römer complex, the house on the left is the **Alt Limpurg**, first mentioned in 1336 as Haus Laderam and rebuilt in Renaissance style in 1595. It adjoins the Römer which is, in turn, attached to the **Haus Löwenstein**. The three gables of these houses are the symbol of Frankfurt. The coats of arms under the balcony are from neighboring cities and territories. Those on the Löwenstein depict eight of the city's noble families.

To the right, the town hall incorporates Haus Frauenstein and the Salzhaus, both rebuilt after the Second World War in 1950s style, with mosaic gables. The other houses making up the complex stretch out from behind. Sometimes one can see wedding parties emerging from the central doorway of the Römer and flower-bedecked cars waiting for them.

Walk around the corner of the Alt Limpurg where you can buy some of Frankfurt's local wine at the **Stadt Weingut**. (Open weekdays 7:30am-4pm.) Enter the little passageway leading to the **Römerhöfchen** with its Hercules Fountain. The coats of arms of Frankfurt's quarters are on the wall. This is where the Imperial processions used to begin. Buy a ticket from the automat there and climb the outdoor staircase, which was built in 1627. Inside are more stairs – the Kaisertreppe which lead to the **Kaisersaal** (Imperial Hall). (Open weekdays 9am-1pm and 1:30-5pm, Sunday 10am-4pm, except during official functions, which take place fairly often. It is best to phone ahead to find out if it is open. Tel. 2124814.)

The hall was first known as the *Römersaal* and served as banquet hall and meeting place for the city council. After 1562, when

*The Römer (the historical old Town Hall) and the allegorical figure of Justice*

the first coronation was held in Frankfurt, it became the Kaisersaal. Goethe describes how he managed to get in – uninvited – to the coronation banquet for Josef II held here.

After Germany lost its Imperial status in 1806, the Städel Art Institute's director came up with the idea of placing the portraits of all 52 Emperors of the German Realm in the hall to commemorate the days of the Empire. The leading portrait artists of the time (Rethel, Steinle, Veith, and Waldmüller) were commissioned to do the work between 1838 and 1853. The life-size oil figures take you through 1,000 years of history, from Charlemagne (768-814) to Franz II (1792-1806). During World War II the paintings were removed for safekeeping and were later replaced in the Gothic niches of the Kaisersaal. The coffered ceiling was restored in 1955 according to the original, which dated from 1612.

Return to the square and face the east side, once called the Saturday Hill (Samstagsberg), where justice was dispensed in medieval times, and which is now known as the **Ostzeile** (eastern part). The impressive half-timbered houses are carefully constructed replicas of the original buildings that were destroyed during the war. Great contro-

*The Eiserner Steg, a walkway across the Main*

versy surrounded their rebuilding, but it was finally accomplished in 1984. The houses have kept their original names: (from the left) Great Angel (Großer Engel) and Little Angel (Kleiner Engel), Golden Griffon (Goldener Greif), Wild Man (Wilder Mann), Little Badger Hill/Key (Kleiner Dachsberg/Schlüssel), Great Gallery (Großer Laubenberg), and Little Gallery (Kleiner Laubenberg).

The group of houses across the square are in the typical style of the 1950s. Across the Saalgasse is the Black Star (Schwarzer Stern). The best restaurant in this section is *Zum Standesämtchen* in the Kleiner Laubenberg.

Beside the Schwarzer Stern is the **Old St. Nicolas Church** (Alte Nikolaikirche). Open daily 9am-8pm. It was built in 1290 and dedicated to the patron of boatmen. From 1460 a watchman was stationed in the tower to greet vessels with a blast of his horn. From the gallery select citizens could watch ceremonies or jousting in the square below. Today sharpshooters are posted there during state visits to the Römer.

Behind the church is the **Historical Museum** (Historisches Museum) located at

*The Historical Museum*

19 Saalgasse. (Open Tues.-Sun. 10am-5pm, Wed. 10am-8pm, Tel. 212-35599.) Its collections were saved from the destruction of World War II, and the museum was reopened in 1972 in the Baroque Saalhof, with the addition of a modern front. The small chapel of the Emperor Frederik Barbarossa inside was built in the 12th century and is the oldest structure in Frankfurt.

The museum not only preserves relics from Frankfurt's interesting history, but also serves as a dynamic information center. History becomes more accessible through graphic film, slide, and other sophisticated presentations. In the new building the exhibits are displayed in chronological order.

Of particular interest are two models of the city of Frankfurt. Near the entrance is a model of what remained of the city's core on the morning of March 24, 1944, after a bombing raid by American and British air forces. Because most of the houses were wooden, the bombs created a fire that engulfed most of what had been a beautiful medieval city. Only *Haus Wertheym*, facing the museum, remained reasonably intact, perhaps because it was the headquarters of the fire brigade...

Across the courtyard is a room of baroque sculptures. The other model of Frankfurt, as it stood in 1927 is housed here. Houses constructed half of timber are crowded together in the narrow alleyways and the Römerberg square seems more spacious than it is today.

The Graphics Collection on the ground floor has information exhibits illustrating the city's growth. Coin collectors will be interested in the coin cabinet (*Münzkabinett*) but will have to get permission to see it. A children's museum is also located here. On the second floor is a costume collection from the 18th to 20th centuries. The museum often presents films and lectures, and jazz bands sometimes perform on Sunday mornings in summer.

The museum has a cafeteria, but it is more pleasant to have a beer and a meal at *Haus Wertheym*, across the way from the museum.

*Haus Wertheym* is a typical German *Gaststätte* (inn). It serves large portions of traditional food, specializing in schnitzels, which go well with draught beer – a very strong, dark *Eisbock*. There is a valuable collection of beer steins that guests can admire, and humorous signs, some in English, that clutter the room.

After a refreshing German lunch it is always a good idea to go for a walk, especially if the weather is nice. As you exit *Haus Wertheym* you will be in just right place to begin a pleasant walk along the **Mainkai**, the promenade along the Main River. It gives a superb view of Museum Row opposite, the barge, and pleasure boat traffic.

Start at the Fahrtor, which meets the Mainkai at the Rententurm. Notice the flood-level markings on the tower. The **Eiserner Steg** (Iron Bridge), a pedestrian walkway, crosses the Main here to Sachsenhausen. Opened as a toll bridge in the mid-19th century, it was blown up in World

War II, and rebuilt with red sandstone, like the original. This is the best spot to listen to the ringing of the church bells during Christmas, or to watch fireworks on the river and the jousting of the boatmen during the Main Fest in August.

At the foot of the bridge are the landings for cruise ships, (which operate from Easter to mid-October), and the stop for the Historical Steam Train, which makes short excursions on some weekends throughout the year.

Walk along the Mainkai to **St. Leonard's Church** (Leonhardskirche). (Open Tues.-Fri. 3-6pm, Sat. 9am-noon and 3-6pm, Sunday 9am-1pm and 3-6pm.) The entrance is on Alter Mainzer Gasse.

When it was founded in 1219, the church was dedicated to the Saints Mary and George, but it was rededicated when it acquired the relics of St. Leonard in 1323. The northern doorway, dating back to 1220, still survives from the original structure. Notice the figures of Christ with the Virgin Mary and Saints John, George, and Peter in the tympanum above the doorway.

The church was completed only shortly before the Reformation, but it had already

*St. Leonard's Church*

fallen into disrepair by the early 16th century. Restoration began in 1808. The five windows of the choir contain fragments of Gothic stained glass. Holbein's *Last Supper* which you see here is a copy, the original of which is in the Städel Art Institute. The *Altar of the Virgin* is 16th-century Flemish work, and the carved Bavarian High Altar dates from about 1500. Flood levels are marked on the wall beneath the organ balcony.

Tucked between Karmelitergasse and Seckbächer Gasse is

*A view from the top of the Dom's tower*

the **Karmeliterkloster** (Carmelite Cloister). It can be reached from St. Leonard's along Alter Mainzer Gasse; or take the long way around on the Mainkai and enter through the Gothic arch on the right.

The cloister was rebuilt in the late 1950s and houses the **Municipal Archives**. Its great treasure is a copy of the *Golden Bull*, the edict Emperor Charles IV issued in 1356, making Frankfurt the site of Imperial elections. A few years ago the fine Renaissance refectory was restored and the cloister was glassed in to protect its fading 16th-century paintings. The artist Jörg Ratgeb is responsible for two cycles of frescoes that depict the story of the Carmelite Order and of Christ's nativity and passion. His fine work, however, did not prevent him from being hanged, drawn and quartered after leading a peasant revolt in 1526.

The cloister is housing the **Museum of Pre- and Early History** (Museum für Vor- und Frühgeschichte), 1 Karmelitergasse, Tel. 212-35896. Open Tues.-Sun. 10am-5pm, Wed. 10am-8pm. The archeological history of Frankfurt is exhibited here and there are special exhibits for the blind and visually handicapped.

Return to the Mainkai and cross the busy street to the green bank of the river. At 14 Untermainkai, the **Rothschild Palais** houses the **Jewish Museum** (Jüdisches Museum). Open Tues.-Sun. 10am-5pm, Wed.

10am-8pm. The site was the home of the famous banking family. Nearby, the Chinese restaurant *Nizza*, has a roof-top terrace where you can relax and enjoy the view. From here you can either take a relaxing stroll along the embankment to Nizza Anlage or cross over the Eiserner Steg into Alt-Sachsenhausen.

**Nizza Anlage** is so named because the landscape here is reminiscent of the French resort Nice. Gingko, lemon, almond and fig trees give it an almost Mediterranean air. The sundial here was a gift from the Heddernheim Copper Works and the old crane remains from the winter harbor which was formerly on this site.

*The Römerberg, a center of public life in Frankfurt*

## The Left Bank of the Main – Applewine in Alt-Sachsenhausen

Alt-Sachsenhausen is a little triangle
timbered houses. This is where the vill
but it is by no means all of this very l
believed that Charlemagne founded S
defeated Saxons. Sachsenhausers, at
Sachsenhausers first and Frankfurters s
the quarter was incorporated into Fran
within the city walls. The Stadtwald (
hausen and three-quarters of Sachsenha

Alt-Sachsenhausen, however, is very
prettied-up half-timbered houses, bar
against one another. The area's old-fashi
cobbled lanes and greenery give it a me

It can be reached on foot from the Eise
Steg, by Bus 36 or 46, or Straßenbahn
16, or 17. Approach from the Eiserner S
stopping for a look first at the **Three Ki
Church** (Dreikönigskirche) overlooking
river. Its spire rises nearly 80 meters.
first major neo-Gothic church built in Fra
furt, it was designed by Franz Josef
Denzinger, who also completed the Cat
dral. The church replaced a chapel that
been founded on the site in 1340. Nearby
a neoclassical fountain and sculpture of

*[handwritten margin notes: LEFT BANK. (2) ALT-SACHSENHAUSEN APPLEWINE]*

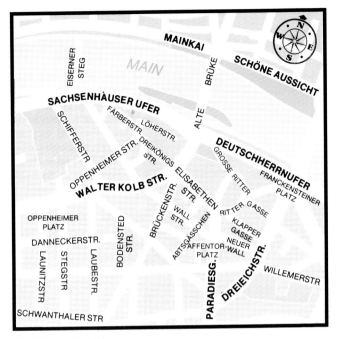

**SACHSENHAUSEN**

Three Kings dating from 1781. The fountain replaced a medieval well.

A good restaurant here is *Maaschanz*, at 75 Färberstraße.

Walk along Dreikönigstraße to the very short Schellgasse. At no. 8 is the oldest half-timbered house in Germany, one of 4,000 half-timbered houses in Frankfurt. It was a *Rauchhaus* (smoke house), where meat was

preserved by being hung from the rafters and smoked, a practice that also helped preserve the wood.

Continue to the major thoroughfare Walter-Kolb-Straße, named for the first elected lord mayor (*Oberbürgermeiste*r) after the war. Walk back in the direction of the river to the **Deutschordenshaus**, a baroque structure of the Teutonic Order, an organization of knights. It stands on the site of an earlier Gothic house. (Open Mon.-Fri. 9am-5pm, except Wed. 9am-8pm.) Three wings were designed by Daniel Kayser. Erected between 1709 and 1715, it was destroyed in the 1944 bombing and rebuilt, with some changes, between 1963 and 1965. A few original pieces remain, including figures of knights from 1715 by Erich Neuberger of Idstein; coats of arms dating back to 1565, which can be seen in the southern courtyard; the *Virgin* by Bernhard Schwarzburger at the northwestern corner, and a capital from about 1200 on the neo-Gothic presbytery.

The Teutonic Order owned the building until 1958. It now houses municipal offices of the arts and sciences. Exhibitions by local artists are sometimes mounted here.

Beside it is **St. Mary's Church** (St. Mariakirche), with some fine Gothic side altars and a wooden sculpted depiction of the *Beheading of John the Baptist*, also dating back to the Gothic period. The church's baroque facade was completed in 1751 to harmonize with its neighbor.

*The Kuhhirtenturm, a watch tower at the heart of Alt-Sachsenhausen*

Continue in the direction of the river to Deutschherrnufer. There is a youth hostel just down the street, but you will turn onto Große Rittergasse just before you reach it. The tower before you is the **Kuhhirtenturm** (Cowherd's Tower). Built in 1490, it is the only surviving watch tower of five within the Sachsenhausen fortifications. The composer Paul Hindemith lived here from 1923-27, during the time he was director of the Frankfurt Opera House.

This is the heart of Alt Sachsenhausen. Wander along the streets until you find a bar or applewine pub that suits your fancy. You will recognize applewine pubs by the evergreen wreaths over the doors. (For more about Frankfurt's national drink, see "Wining and Dining.")

Finally, take Neuer Wall or Paradiesgasse to the **Affentorplatz**. This is the center of many Sachsenhausen festivals, including the Brunnen Fest in late August.

An old Guard and Customs House from 1810 stands in this square, along with more applewine pubs. The edifice was part of Frankfurt's defence facilities, but the name is a bit mystifying. In 1350, a *Haus zum Affen* (Ape House) stood there, but its name may originally have been Ave-Tor. In 1809, it was known as Aschaffenburger Tor, sitting as it does on the road to Aschaffenburg. The Affenbrunnen (Monkey Fountain) is modern.

On Saturday you may wish to wander over to the *Schlachthof* (slaughter house) toward the **Flea Market** (*Flohmarkt*). Take Bus 36, or walk, from the Lokalbahnhof to Wendelplatz.

There is another hike up the hill to the **Henninger Tower** (Henninger Turm), 60-64 Hainer Weg, the grain elevator or tower of the Henninger Brewery. There is a parking lot at the brewery for those who drive. The tower has two revolving restaurants – try to get a table by the windows. Open Tues.-Sun. 10am-11pm. There is also a viewing platform and a small **Brewing Museum** (open until 7pm). At 120 meters (approximately 350 feet), the tower provides the best view of Frankfurt. On clear days, you can see as far as the Taunus Range behind the

TV tower. There is a charge for the elevator, but the climb up 731 steps is free. A souvenir shop can be found on the ground floor.

Nearby, enter **Sachs**, an underground mini-Frankfurt, from Darmstädter Landstraße. The well-known pubs and cafés of the city have been recreated here, but the atmosphere is as phoney as the rock buildings. Drinks are expensive, the music is loud, and there is a cover charge. The only worthwhile site is the cavernous cellar of the brewery in which it is built. Open evenings only and closed Sunday.

*Enjoying applewine in Sachsenhausen*

Sachsenhäuser Berg is a well-to-do neighborhood of new single-family houses and high-rise apartment buildings. The *Holiday Inn* is on the Darmstädter Landstraße, and a little farther along at 279 Darmstädter Landstraße is the **Sachsenhäuser Warte**, a post-Gothic watch tower dating from 1471, which was part of the old outer defences. Inside are the remains of a baroque forester's lodge built in 1767. It is now a pub and restaurant with open-air seating at long tables.

## Museum Row and Surroundings – A Cultural Feast

Museum Row can be reached by Bus 46 or by U-Bahn 1, 2 or 3 to Theaterplatz or Schweizer Platz. Drivers can find streetside parking at the Friedensbrücke end of the row if they arrive early. We suggest beginning at this end for two other reasons. To begin, the small café in the Liebieghaus serves delicious homemade *torte* (what better way to start the day?). In addition, it will be convenient for you to either go to Alt-Sachsenhausen as it begins to liven up for the evening or to wander around Schweizer Straße.

The Schaumainkai, a major road which runs along the Main between the Eiserner Steg and the Friedensbrücke, has another name – *Museumsufer* (Museum Row). Facing the river are seven museums, from the stark-white Museum of Applied Arts (Museum für Kunsthandwerk) to the old villa, the Liebieghaus (Museum of Sculpture). In between come the Ethnographic Museum (Museum für Völkerkunde), the German Film Museum (Deutsches Filmmuseum), the German Museum of Architecture (Deutsches Architekturmuseum), the German Postal Museum (Deutsches Postmuseum), and the Städel Art Institute and Municipal Gallery (Städelsches Kunstinstitut und Städtische Galerie), simply known as the Städel.

It would take an entire day to make even a cursory visit to all these museums, so we suggest that you pick those whose subjects interest you, and stroll past the others. All the museums are closed on Monday, and most stay open until 8pm on Wednesday.

*A sculpture lesson in Frankfurt*

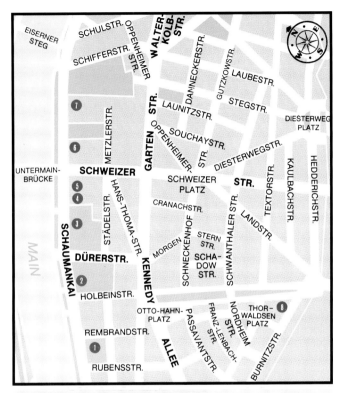

## MUSEUM ROW AND SURROUNDINGS

1. Liebieghaus
2. Städel
3. Bundespostmuseum
4. Deutsches Architekturmuseum
5. Deutsches Filmmuseum
6. Museum für Völkerkunde
7. Museum für Kunsthandwerk
8. Bonifatiuskirche

As you walk along the embankment pause for a look at Frankfurt's skyline. Some people liken it to Chicago's and yet others call it "Mainhatten." You may wish to wander along the green area beside the river or, if the weather is good, take a trip on one of the pedal boats, which you can rent near the Eiserner Steg during the summer.

The **Liebieghaus** is located at 71 Schaumainkai (open Tues.-Sun. 10am-5pm, Wed. until 8pm, Tel. 212-38617). The edifice is a late nineteenth-century villa designed in the style of a fortified manor house. The city acquired it to house a museum of sculpture and added the gallery wing in 1909. The facade of this wing reflects the local penchant for mixing baroque and *Jugendstil* (art nouveau) styles. It contains works from ancient Egypt, Asia, Greece and Rome, as well as examples of European sculpture from the Middle Ages, the Renaissance and the baroque and rococo periods.

The **Städel**, at 63 Schaumainkai, could take an entire day in itself. (Open Tues.-Sun. 10am-5pm, Wed. until 8pm, Tel. 605098-0.) The collections represents all European periods; 600 years of art from Italian Fra Angelico to Paul Klee. Buy a museum map at the front desk to find the exhibits you wish to see. Do not miss Tischbein's *Goethe in Campagna* at the top of the stairs.

The Städel Art Institute was founded in 1816 with the collection of 474 pictures that local banker Johann Friedrich Städel left to the city. Along with the pictures came a fortune of one million British florins to assist in establishing an art institute. To house it, the city erected the present building between 1874 and 1878. Architect Oskar Sommer, who also built the Stock

*Strolling along the bank of the Main*

*The entrance to the German Postal Museum*

Exchange, designed the building in the style of the Louvre.

The State College of Art has been a part of the Institute almost since its inception.

In addition to the European collection, the Städel has a graphics section with some 25,000 drawings and 65,000 prints. The **Galerie** (Gallery), a separate entity housed in the same building, includes works of the nineteenth and twentieth centuries. Excellent exhibitions are displayed regularly, for which there is a separate charge.

The **German Postal Museum** (Deutsches Postmuseum) is at 53 Schaumainkai, Tel. 60600. (Open Tues.-Sun. 10am-5pm, Wed. 10am-8pm.) The museum displays the history of communications in Germany and the international development of telecommunications.

The German Postal Museum exhibits stamps, of course, but it has much more than that: ornate old mailboxes, post-coach driver's uniforms, and old-fashioned telephones. All these convey the history of communications. But the museum does not only depict the past – a model of a satellite contrasts with a wooden drum once used by African tribes to send messages. A modern-day telephone exchange lights up as you dial to show just what happens inside the wires.

The **German Museum of Architecture** (*Deutsches Architekturmuseum*, DAM for short), is situated at 43 Schaumainkai. (Open Tues.-Sun. 10am-5pm, Wed. until 8pm. Tel. 21238471.) The German Museum of Architecture is Germany's only museum on the subject of architecture. Drawings, models, photos etc and special exhibits are shown during the year. It is a house within a house within a house, all packaged in a big glass block. Its construction was a difficult urban-landscape project that was executed by New York architect Oswald Mathias Ungers. He left the shell of the original villa, building in and around it. Models, plans, sketches, and urban panoramas make up most of the exhibits. There are also various changing shows.

*The Museum of Architecture and the Film Museum standing side by side*

A coffee shop connects the German Museum of Architecture with the **German Film Museum** (Deutsches Filmmuseum) at no. 41. (Open Tues.-Sun. 10am-5pm, Wed.

*The Museum of Applied Arts*

10am-8pm. Tel. 21238830.) The displays trace German films and filming equipment, and let the visitor experiment with magic lanterns and other early entertainment gadgets. The book shop offers are fine variety of art, film, and architecture books and posters. A library and special exhibitions hall are also housed in the museum.

The *Kommunales Kino* (movie theater) operates in conjunction with the museum, showing classics from all over the world, often in their original language or with subtitles in English. Daily 5:30-8pm.

Cross the busy Schweizer Straße to the **Ethnological Museum** (Museum für Völkerkunde) at 29 Schaumainkai. The museum curators have had to cope with lack of space here since the former home of the exhibits, the Palais Thurn and Taxis, was bombed in 1944. (Open Tues.-Sun. 10am-5pm, Wed. until 8pm. Tel. 21235391.) They have handled the problem of displaying the collection of approximately 52,000 items by providing changing exhibitions instead of permanent displays. The exhibits focus on the history and culture of the Third World. The museum serves as an information center for exploring the destructive influences of Imperialism and neo-colonialism on the cultural and economic systems of Africa,

Latin America, and the South Sea Islands. Each exhibition is the product of exhaustive research, and is detailed in a booklet (in German only).

A large park with footpaths and a fountain connects this museum to the newest one of the Row, the **Museum of Applied Arts** (Museum für Kunsthandwerk) at 17 Schaumainkai. (Open Tues.-Sun. 10am-5pm, Wed. until 8pm. Tel. 21234037. Admission free except for special exhibits.) Designed by the American architect Richard Meyer, the building won the 1978 Honor Award given by The American Institute of Architects. It is connected by a glassed-in bridge to the Villa Metzler, which originally housed the collection. The neoclassical villa was built between 1802 and 1804 and was renovated extensively in 1865.

The main building is angular and full of light, and together with the other buildings house some 30,000 specimens of craftsmanship from Europe and Asia, spanning from the Middle Ages to the twentieth century. The collection of Jugendstil (art nouveau) furniture is particularly good, as is the goldsmith work. The ground floor café has a beautiful terrace, which is a real treat on sunny days.

From here its an easy walk back to Schweizer Straße. This is a wonderful place to stroll around or to relax in an applewine pub after a stimulating day at the museums.

*An appetizing array of delicacies in a Frankfurt shop*

Schweizer Straße is the glamour street of Sachsenhausen. It can be reached by Bus 46 or the U-1, 2 or 3 to Schweizer Platz or the Südbahnhof.

Running straight from the river, it is lined with expensive boutiques, butcher shops, and applewine pubs.

It curves in the middle at Schweizerplatz, where streets radiate in all directions. This is the center of nineteenth century Sachsenhausen, an area of charming row houses, most of which have been turned into luxury apartments.

Two of the most popular applewine pubs are here – *Wagner* at no. 71 and the *Gemälter Haus* at no. 67. Look at the florid wall decor before you enter. The pub boasts standing-room only on weekend nights, but it is worth trying to crowd onto one of the long benches during that time.

There is a good beer house next door to *Wagner*. The *Palais des Bieres*, at the corner of Textorstraße, has better decor than beer. For dinner, try an expensive, but delicious meal at the *Gans* at 76 Schweizer Straße, or the *Bistro Empor* at 8 Schneckenhofstraße, also high-priced and tasty. Two good cafés on Schweizer Straße are *Café Will* at no. 59, where you can get breakfast until 2pm, and the *Südcafé* at no. 90.

Almost at the end of the street, before the railroad bridge, turn east on Hedderichstraße and walk past the school to Diesterwegplatz. The **Südbahnhof** (South Railway Station) stands on one side; it is a major interchange for buses, trains, Straßenbahnen and the U-Bahn. Many surrounding towns can be reached from here.

*In Frankfurt, art is displayed in non-conventional places as well*

Facing the station are a few nice shops and a large post office where you can change money. Recommended among these stores are *Freyberg* for blouses and the *Salatschüssel* for good take-out food and fancy kitchen gadgets.

The area west of Schweizer Straße is mostly a quiet residential area, with a group of "artist streets" – Rembrandtstraße, Rubensstraße, Tischbeinstraße and Holbeinstraße which leads to the Städel. The **Bonifatius Church** (Bonifatiuskirche) at no. 70 Holbeinstraße was constructed in 1920, and was built with clinker brick by Martin Weber.

A pleasant excursion to the eastern edge of Sachsenhausen is to the **Gerber Mill** (Gerbermühle). The inn at the mill serves some of the best applewine in Frankfurt. Sit on the front lawn and watch the river traffic flow by. The ride to the inn is pleasant, either by car via Deutschherrnufer (the parking lot is often crowded) or by Bus 46. An even better way to get there in summer is on one of the excursion boats which go upstream as far as the Gerbermühle and pause at the small landing stage there.

*Statues at the yard of the Liebieghaus*

## The Right Bank of the Main – History Amidst Modernity

Retrace your steps on your way to exploring the western side. From the Römerberg, cross Braubachstraße, across from the Technical Town Hall.

At Paulsplatz is the **St. Paul's Church** (Paulskirche), which is closely linked with Frankfurt's – and all Germany's – fortunes. Established in 1271 by the Franciscans, the church was used as a library and a school after the Reformation. It eventually became the city's main Protestant place of worship. Its importance, however, lies more in its secular history.

On May 18, 1848, the German National Assembly took over the building. Although their attempts to unify the various German states were stopped by the emperor, the church remains the symbol of hope for freedom and unity among the Germans. U.S. President John F. Kennedy spoke here on his visit to Frankfurt. It is here that the publishing industry awards its *Friedenspreis* (peace prize) during the annual Frankfurt Book Fair and this is where the ceremonies are held for the Goethe Prize, for the Theodor W. Adorno Prize (for sociology and philosophy), for the Otto Hahn Prize (for the peaceful use of atomic energy), and for the Paul-Ehrlich Prize (for cancer research). The Goethe Award is, perhaps, most highly esteemed. Among its recipients are famous figures such as Albert Schweitzer, Sigmund Freud, Hermann Hesse and Ingmar Bergman.

It took 44 years (1789-1833) to build the original red sandstone structure. During the Second World War the church served as a

*St. Paul's Church, closely linked with Germany's fortunes*

refuge for a Protestant resistance group. It was destroyed in the 1944 bombings but was quickly rebuilt "in stone as in spirit". Only in 1988 the church was renovated, and is open for visits, congresses, and exhibitions.

The Unity Monument stands in the Paulsplatz. Down Braubachstraße, there are several good antiques shops and art galleries.

Beside the church, a short pedestrian street, Neue Kräme, leads past Italian cafés and traditional bratwurst stands to Berliner Straße. This used to be the old town prior to the bombings. It is long and straight, lined with blocks of buildings put up hastily at a time when people needed housing and money was scarce. There is talk of beautifying the street, but preservationists are trying to save this rather ugly area as an example of 1950s architecture.

*The Church of Our Lady*

Continue along Neue Kräme to the **Liebfrauenberg**. This square used to be the site of a horse and cattle fair in the fourteenth and fifteenth centuries. Many of Frankfurt's homeless gather on this square, but it is also an area of shops and cafés.

On one side of the square stands the **Church of Our Lady** (Liebfrauenkirche), founded as a Lady Chapel in 1310. Building was begun in 1318 and the church continued to grow well into the nineteenth century. It was damaged in the war and rebuilt in 1954.

The tympanum of the Three Kings Doorway depicts the *Adoration of the Shepherds and the Three Kings*. The half-length figures are the prophets Jeremiah and Isaiah. In the porch is a *Pieta*, dating from 1383. The magnificent Rococo interior was destroyed

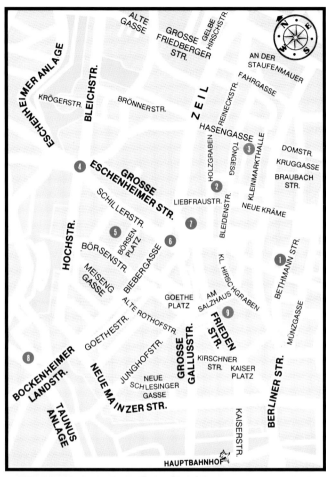

**RIGHT BANK OF THE MAIN**

1. *Pauluskirche*
2. *Liebfrauenkirche*
3. *Kleinmarkthalle*
4. *Eschenheimer Turm*
5. *Börse*
6. *Hauptwache*
7. *Katharinenkirche*
8. *Alte Oper*
9. *Goethe Haus*

in the war, except for the altar figures by Johann Jakob Juncker. When the church was rebuilt the Gothic vaulted ceiling was replaced by a flat timber roof.

Now turn back along the Ziegelgasse to the

small market (Kleinmarkthalle), which is open during regular business hours. This bustling covered food market is built on two levels. Almost every sort of fruit and vegetable you could possibly want is available here, from California grapefruit to zucchini blossoms that the Italians dip in batter and fry. Upstairs are a number of Turkish stalls where you can enjoy some good lamb.

The main entrance to the market is on Hasengasse, which leads to the Zeil, but we will walk along Töngesgasse to the **Staufen Walls** (Staufenmauer) – the remains of the twelfth century city walls. New fortifications were constructed in the fourteenth century and most of the Staufen Walls were eventually pulled down. The Wollgraben on the east side of town was assigned to the Jews as a ghetto. It all but completely burned down in 1711, and the residents were forced to rebuild the part of the wall that was destroyed. This is the part of the wall that still stands.

From here you can take Fahrgasse to the Konstablerwache, and continue up to the Zeil.

The **Zeil**, the country's richest shopping street, runs from Friedberger Anlage to the Hauptwache, but you will be most interested in concentrating on the pedestrian zone between the Konstablerwache and the Hauptwache. S-Bahnen 1, 2, 3, 4, 5, 6 and 14; U-Bahnen 6 and 7 reach this point. The Konstablerwache can also be reached by U-4 and U-5 and bus 36 and 30.

The **Konstablerwache** is a large developed square where festivals are held and which young boys use as a skateboard arena. It is surrounded by shops and office buildings, which stretch

*The Zeil in winter*

*A street performance on the Zeil*

down along the pedestrian zone (*Fußgängerzone*) of the Zeil. This is where you can find the big department stores, as well as a number of leather and shoe shops. Several cafés and beer bars are set up in the center of the wide street, but these are expensive and not particularly good. A better choice is one of the department store restaurants.

The Zeil is always crowded with shoppers, office workers, street artists, beggars and vendors selling soft pretzels or cheap jewelry. The modern fountains are turned on in summer, and are a favorite meeting place for young people, both students and spiky-haired punks.

The main post office is on this street. Walk around the corner at the big department store *Kaufhof* onto Große Eschenheimer Straße for a look at the telecommunications center. This is the site of the old **Palace of the Thurn and Taxis Families** (Palais Thurn und Taxis). The family became wealthy as Imperial Postmasters in the days of the Empire. They built a magnificent baroque palace here, and when they moved to Regensburg, it was used as a postal building. It was destroyed in World War II and only the entrance was restored in original style. The figure of Minerva bears the family coat of arms. The **telecommunications house** (Fernmeldehochhaus) here is the largest in Germany. It also has international radio and television links.

At the end of Große Eschenheimer Straße, on an island in the middle of ring-road traffic, is the **Eschenheimer Tower** (Eschenheimer Turm). It was part of the medieval defence system and is a fine example of Late Gothic style. It was built between 1400 and 1428 by the architect who designed the Cathedral tower, Madern Gerthener. It is probably his portrait you see on the arch underneath the sentry walk. Above the walk is the Frankfurt Eagle that

*The Eschenheimer Tower, which used to be part of the city's medieval defence system*

*The Hauptwache, a popular coffee house, and St. Catherine's Church*

he carved. A gilded weather vane tops the tower. It is believed that a convicted poacher, Hans Winkelsee, purchased his life by making it.

The tower is in poor condition and cannot be entered. Return to the Zeil along the Schillerstraße. The **Stock Exchange** (Börse) is on your right at 6 Börsenplatz. (Tours are available Mon.-Fri. at 10, 11 and 12am.) It is Germany's largest stock exchange. The *Börsenkeller*, a large restaurant in the cellar of the Exchange, is a favorite dining place for Frankfurters. The vegetarian restaurant *Eden* is behind the Exchange on Rahmhofstraße.

Schillerstraße ends at the **Hauptwache**, whose Rococo style belies its former use as the city's main guard house and jail. In fact, it has been a café since 1904, and now that the venerable *Kranzler Café* across the square has been turned into a steak-and-salad restaurant, the *Hauptwache* is doubly popular for afternoon coffee and *Torte*. Behind the building is the neo classical Hauptwache Fountain (Hauptwache-Brunnen). It was erected at the beginning of the nineteenth century to replace a Renaissance well.

On the south side of the square, standing at an angle to the Hauptwache, is the **St. Catherine's Church** (Katherinenkirche), where Goethe was baptized and confirmed. The first Protestant sermon preached in Frankfurt was delivered here in 1522 by Hartmann Ibach. The church was destroyed in 1944, and rebuilding was completed ten years later with a simplified interior. The principal attractions are the 15 stained glass windows by Carl Crodel. Its organ is the largest in the city, with 4,400 pipes. It is an obvious venue, therefore, for sacred music concerts.

*Busy Frankfurt. Opposite the end of the Zeil is the St. Catherine's Church*

The square is called An der Hauptwache and the passage beneath it is a busy junction of the S- and U-Bahnen. The passage is filled with shops and snack bars and extends to the Freßgass'. Before going underground take a look at the Struwwelpeter Fountain, a monument to the children's story character created by Frankfurt doctor Heinrich Hoffmann.

Proceed along the Freßgass'. From the Hauptwache, go along the Steinweg to

Rathenauplatz, which joins the **Goetheplatz**. A good place to relax over lunch, is the *Restaurant Goetheplatz*.

Cross Börsenstraße. If you are looking for reading material, most of the bookshops in the area have English-language paperbacks. The *British Bookshop* down the street at 17 Börsenstraße has the largest selection.

*The Freßgass'*, "Grazing Alley", is the nickname for the pedestrian zone of Kalbächer Gasse and Große Bockenheimer Straße because of all the restaurants and food shops that line it. During the Wine Festival in August, vintagers set up booths and dispense wine in small taster's glasses or by the bottle. The *Weihenstephan* beer house serves beer from the "oldest brewery in the world" (the brewery is in Bavaria). The *Café Schwille*, about halfway along, is a well-established place for pastries or a light lunch. It is attached to a small hotel.

Children love the fountain on this street; the statue of the larger-than-life reclining woman is their favorite.

*The majestic Alte Oper*

DEM WAHREN SCHOENEN GUTEN

Come out at the Opernplatz and the reborn **Alte Oper** (Old Opera House). In front of the Opera House is the Marshall Fountain (*Marschall-Brunnen*), named in honor of the originator of the Marshall Plan, which helped put Germany back on its feet after World War II.

*The façade of the Alte Oper, with its classic decorative carvings*

Take note of the incredible view from here – the Alte Oper in the foreground with the SGZ Bank skyscraper behind and, in the distance, the needle-thin Telecommunications Tower (Fernmeldeturm). The tower is the highest in West Germany at 330 meters (approximately 980 ft.), and on foggy days its tip disappears altogether.

The original Italian High Renaissance Alte Oper was so sumptuous that it rivaled those in Dresden and Paris. Emperor Wilhelm I was guest of honor for the grand opening on 20th October, 1880, a glittering affair that must have rivaled the coronations of earlier days.

Mozart's *Don Juan* was performed for the occasion, a tribute to the composer who won the city's heart when he performed there as a child of seven.

The original seating capacity of the opera house was relatively small, just 1,800, and well-to-do citizens who had contributed to the building fund received the choice seats. Among those who performed there was Caruso, who appeared every year from 1908 to 1911.

*The skyscrapers of the Deutsche Bank rising above the "green belt"*

The building was destroyed during the bombing in March 1944. For years, controversy raged about how to rebuild it. In the end, its exterior was restored, but the interior was broken up into concert halls and meeting rooms, and the grand staircase was not rebuilt. The Alte Oper reopened in 1981. Activities at the Opera include jazz, rock, folk, and chamber music performances, as well as seminars and conferences. Senior citizens and young people are catered for, and several different activities take place at the same time. Every Friday night there is Dixieland music in the Opernkeller (cellar).

Several restaurants and cafés can be found in the building. The *Jacques Offenbach Restaurant* at the underground ticket-window level is very good (go down the outside circular steps that also lead to the parking garage). A number of cafés and restaurants on the square cater to the yuppie crowd, and the *Mövenpick Restaurant* across the way is one of the better eateries in Frankfurt. It is divided into several sections – you may prefer the quiet dining rooms to the café or grill-counter areas. *Baron de la Mouette* is the best. There is also an outdoor terrace and, in the summer, an ice-cream carousel.

The "green belt" running along the ring road follows the crescent of the old fortifications. It stretches out in front of and behind the Alte Oper. During the day the parks are full of business people from the surrounding banks and offices. After dark, however, stay away as the space is taken over by drug addicts and dealers.

From the Opera, stroll back toward the Hauptwache along Goethestraße, a street of boutiques selling *haute-couture* and expensive jewelry. This is where you find the big-name designers – *Cartier*, *St. Laurent*, etc. A worthwhile detour is into the narrow Kleine Bockenheimer Straße.

Two popular jazz clubs are on this street – the *Jazz Keller*, began as a jazz hideout during the Nazi era, and the *Jazzhaus*, a tiny two-story bar in an historic half-timbered house. The performances in the first is live. The cover charge varies. Music in the *Jazzhaus* is recorded, but very good. If you sit upstairs, you will be asked to lean over the balcony to order drinks, pull them up in a basket, and pay by sending the money down the same way. Goethestraße ends at Börsenstraße.

*Goethe Monument – a tribute to the city's favorite son*

We are now at the Goetheplatz, named for Frankfurt's favorite son. The Rossmarkt (Horse Market) stretches between the Hauptwache and the Goetheplatz and is another good shopping area. From here, walk over to Am Salzhaus. *Onkel Max am Salzhaus* is a good restaurant if you feel like something to eat. Turn onto Großer Hirschgraben to visit the **Goethehaus** (Goethe House) and **Goethe Museum** at No. 23 and 25. (Open Mon.-Sat. 9am-6pm; from October-March until 4pm, Sun. 10am-1pm. Tel. 282824.)

Großer Hirschgraben is a filled-in moat that ran along the first city walls and takes its name from the deer park that once occupied the site.

**Goethehaus** at 23 Großer Hirschgraben is a reconstruction of the house in which Goethe was born. The original home was destroyed in the 1944 bombing. It is furnished in the correct eighteenth century style of late baroque, but few of the contents actually

*The Deutsche Bank*

belonged to the Goethe family. The adjoining **Goethe Museum** contains 14 rooms of documents and displays that depict the life and times of the great poet and philosopher. The exhibits include busts and paintings of Goethe's contemporaries during his younger days, German landscapes and cityscapes, Goethe's journey to Italy, and portraits of the aging Goethe. The Goethe Library contains about 125,000 volumes and a manuscript collection of more than 30,000 signed documents.

Großer Hirschgraben ends at Berliner Straße. Turn right, then right again onto Bethmannstraße. The street is named for Simon Moritz von Bethmann, who turned his family's Frankfurt banking house into an international concern. As a diplomat, he persuaded Napoleon not to march his troops into the city. He is most loved as a philanthropist, a patron of the arts and promoter of social welfare. Little marzipan candies called *Bethmännchen* are still sold in Frankfurt's confectionary shops. The little balls have three slivers of almond set into the sides, representing the sons of Bethmann. Originally, there were four pieces of almond, but when his son Heinrich died in 1845, the number was reduced.

The **Bethmannhof** at the corner of Buchgasse and Bethmannstraße remains headquarters of the banking house Gebrüder

Bethmann. The *Frankfurter Hof*, one of the city's best hotels, stands on Bethmannstraße. Stop for coffee in the lobby-cafe or have an informal grill at the *Frankfurter Stubb*. Alternatively, an excellent choice for a good meal is *Restaurant Français*.

Now stroll down Friedenstraße, past more good shops, to the **Theaterplatz**. On one side of the square the BfG building soars skyward. It houses the Ladengalerie am Theater, a luxurious shopping center, and a good Italian restaurant, *La Galleria*.

On the other side of the square is the **Municipal Theaters** (Städtische Bühnen). It is actually three theaters in one: the Large House (Großes Haus), the Small House (Kleines Haus), and the Intimate Theater (Kammertheater). The modern building (1951-53) is rather stark, with large stretches of glass. Its most valued treasure is the magnificent mural by Marc Chagall that hangs in the foyer.

If you choose not to walk this next stretch, you can reach the Hauptbahnhof (central railway station) by U-Bahn 4 from the Theaterplatz. If you walk, go one block along Neue Mainzer Straße, which is a street of luxury shops including a Mercedes-Benz dealer. To the left, it becomes the city's primary red-light district.

*The Hauptbahnhof (Central Railway Station) with its lavishly decorated façade*

Here you can see many fine old buildings along the street, and as one gets nearer the railway station the area is undergoing cosmetic surgery – new cobblestones and young trees. Although there are plans to move the red-light area to the Ostend (East End), many sex shops and blue movies are still scattered among stores selling cameras, electronic equipment, office supplies, and clothing.

There is an excellent Chinese restaurant, *Tse-Yang*, at 67 Kaiserstraße, about two blocks from the station. A couple of streets away, on Wiesenhüttenplatz, is a small luxury hotel, the *Parkhotel*. Its *Casablanca Bar* is decorated nicely and there is usually a very good piano player.

The **Hauptbahnhof** (Central Railway Station) at the end of the Kaiserstrasse was built under the direction of an architect by the name of Eggert. His plan for a new railway was the winning design in a competition held in 1880. The station took five years to construct, and was, on completion, the largest of its type – a record it maintained for almost thirty years. Note the lavish sculptural decoration on the facade.

*The Zeil*

## The Messe – Trade Fairgrounds

"The Frankfurt Fair had the same significance as the flooding of the Nile in Egypt, except that what it left behind on the banks of the Main was not silt but gold." This analogy is that of Frankfurt chronicler Fried Lübbecke.

He was speaking of the old trade fair on the Römerberg, but he could as easily have been writing about the modern fairs that take place on the Fairgrounds (*Messegelände*). Crowds of exhibitors and visitors surge into the city when a fair begins and recede just as quickly when it is over. The city becomes quiet again, hotel rooms become available and one can get a table at a restaurant without having to make a reservation. Then with the next fair, it starts all over.

The Messe sprawls along Theodor-Heuss-Allee, and is about equidistant from the Hauptbahnhof and the Autobahn West Crossing. It adjoins the main freight rail terminal. The Messe can be reached by Straßenbahn 16 and 19 and Bus 33 and 50.

The Messe was only really developed and expanded after World War II, when the buildings which had been bombed were restored and new ones were built. In recent years the complex has undergone extensive renovations.

The distinctive round building at the City Entrance on Friedrich-Ebert-Anlage is the **Festhalle** (Festival Hall), the grand old lady of the Fairgrounds. When it was built in 1909, it was, at 40 meters (approximately 120 ft.), the largest domed building in Europe. Newly refurbished, it can accommodate 3,000 to 12,000 people. About twice a week, a concert or other event is staged here. It is a favorite spot for visiting rock stars.

*The Festhalle, cornerstone of the Messe*

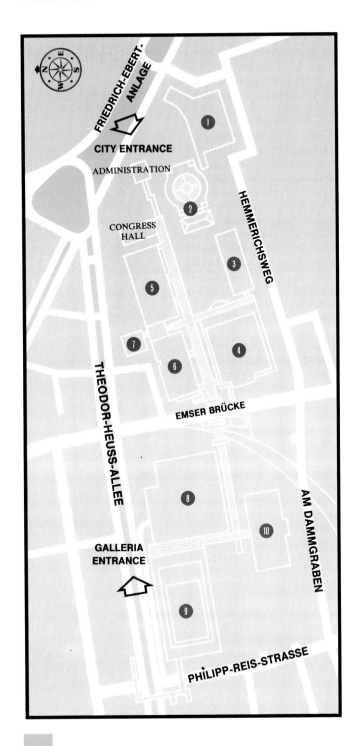

Towering high above the Festhalle is the **Messeturm**, the tallest building in Europe, with 54 floors rising to 253 meters (approximately 760 ft.).

The western entrance is through the **Galleria**, a splendid reception hall stretching almost 100 meters (approximately 300 ft.) under a vaulted glass dome. Stands are never set up here, as it is strictly a meeting place, though it sometimes is used for receptions.

A one kilometer long covered moving walkway, called the *Via Mobile*, connects the buildings, and a small train shuttles visitors free of charge to the ten exhibition halls.

*The 24-story Gate House*

Central to the Messe is the 24-story **Gate House** (Torhaus), built in the form of a gate. It is the administrative center and symbol of the Messe, and has been awarded a national gold medal for architecture and city planning.

The main square, lying between buildings 3 and 5, has been dubbed the **Agora**, an ancient Greek meeting places. Formerly used as open-air exhibition space, it has been planted with trees and lawns to provide a quiet escape from the bustle going on inside the buildings.

The exhibition space is divided into three self-sufficient sections, each of a different size. The main section is made up of Halls 3, 4, and 5. The western unit consists of Halls 8, 9, and 10, including the Galleria, and the eastern unit comprises Hall 1 and the Festhalle. The **Festhalle** is the cornerstone of the Messe. The **Congress Hall** (*Kongresshalle*) is a separate entity and serves as an entrance.

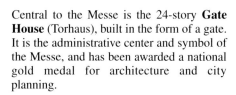

**THE MESSE**

Each of the exhibition halls has its own design. The Kongresshalle is typical of the early 1950s, and was one of the first buildings erected on the Fairgrounds. Its meeting rooms have been given musical names, and there is a *Bräustübl* (beer bar) in the basement, open during fairs. Hall 1 was built in 1950 and has been undergoing renovation.

Hall 3 was rebuilt exactly as it looked in the 1930s, with a high arched roof giving it a barn-like appearance. Hall 4 is glass-walled, making the interior light and airy. It has its own parking garage and is directly connected to Hall 3 and to the Torhaus.

Hall 5 is a two-story building, completed in 1972 to replace several small halls. It is easily recognizable by its projecting stairwells. Its floor are constructed to bear extremely heavy loads.

Hall 6 was designed by the same architect and is the big sister of Hall 5. Functionality was the prime consideration in the design. Hall 7 is another plainly functional building with direct access to Theodor-Heuss-Allee.

*The Messeturm, which rises above the Agora, the main square, and the Festhalle*

Hall 8, constructed in the 1960s, is the largest single-story building on the grounds. It has a natural overhead lighting system, and is directly connected to the Galleria. Hall 9 has the classical red facade of Frankfurt buildings. It was built in the early 1980s, and also has its own parking garage.

Hall 10 is a five-story building containing permanent stands for the Spring and Autumn Fairs – the forerunners of all the Frankfurt fairs. Each exhibitor has designed his own stand, making this a most elegant shopping arcade.

Some 26 restaurants can be found on the grounds, operating during fairs. The food tends to be of the hurry-up-and-eat variety and a bit expensive, but this is an efficient way to serve large crowds.

If you have time, go instead across the street to the *Canadian Pacific Frankfurt Plaza Hotel*, which has an excellent kitchen. The informal *Bäckerei* is less expensive than the *Geheimratsstube*. Another option is to walk down Friedrich-Ebert-Anlage to the *Hessischer Hof Hotel*. This is one of the city's most luxurious hotels, owned by two brother Princes of Hessen. The food is good, and the collection of Sevres porcelain is beautiful.

Note that while many fairs are open to the public, others are for trade visitors only. The Motor Show (IAA) and the Book Fair, both of which take place in Autumn, are among the most important of their kind in the world, and are open to all.

*Enjoying the view seen from the glass-walled Hall 4*

## The Westend – A Desirable Address

The Westend is one of the most highly desired addresses in Frankfurt. It is a quarter of consulates and villas, and lovely old homes that have survived not only the ravages of the war, but also attempts to turn the entire area into a business district. Preservationists have done considerable work, and a number of the old houses have been bought up as *Wohngemeinschaften* (communes) by young people who restored them carefully.

Designed as a garden suburb, Westend is situated between the center of the city and Bockenheim, bordered roughly by the Bockenheimer Warte, Miquelallee, Eschenheimer Landstraße and the city ring road. By the mid-nineteenth century, the gardens were broken up, and villas were built, mostly to the south of Bockenheimer Landstraße. The north side of the large thoroughfare was given over to apartment houses.

It would be impractical to try to walk the entire Westend, though if you wish to wander among some of the streets you may take the U-6 or U-7 to either the Alte Oper or Westend stops and walk about on either side of the Bockenheimer Landstraße. The British Consulate is at No. 51-53.

Some typical streets in the southern area are Feuerbachstraße, Westendstraße, Savignystraße and Guiollettstraße. There is a small *Musikerviertel* (Musicians Quarter) made up of Beethovenstraße, Mendelssohnstraße, Schumannstraße and Schubertstraße.

The small **Heinrich Hoffmann Museum** is at 20 Schubertstraße. (Open Tues.-Sun. 10am-5pm.) Children will enjoy the section that allows them to dress up or play with dolls, games or sound instruments. Adults will appreciate the caricatures of political figures and the English-language book of political poems. The museum is dedicated to Dr. Heinrich Hoffmann, best-known as creator of Struwwelpeter (Slovenly Peter), but also an eminent physician who had advanced ideas about the treatment of the mentally ill.

His character Struwwelpeter was created when Dr. Hoffmann was treating children who were frightened of doctors. To quiet them he would draw pictures of a small boy and would tell them how the boy refused to cut his hair or nails and soon became totally dishevelled. The children were spellbound. As Christmas 1844 drew near, Dr. Hoffmann could not find a book he liked to give his son Carl, so he turned the character into a whole book. Carl loved the book, and soon all the family and friends began to read it. Dr. Hoffmann then wrote more and more stories, mostly with a moral. The museum has a good gift shop and a charming café.

Another Struwwelpeter Museum has opened at 47 Hochstraße.

Attractive streets on the northern side of this quarter are Eppsteinerstraße, Friedrichstraße, Freiherr-von-Stein-Straße and Siesmayerstraße. The last runs along the edge of the Palmengarten, and the U.S. Consulate is situated in an ugly and heavily-guarded building at 21 Siesmayerstraße. The Palmengarten and its neighbor Grüneburg Park are described in the "Parks" section.

In addition to the parks, the main attraction of the Westend is the **Senckenberg Museum of Natural History** (Naturmuseum Senckenberg), one of the best of its kind in Europe. It is found at 25 Senckenberganlage and can be reached by bus 32 and 50. (Open Mon.-Fri. 9am-5pm, Wed. until 8pm, Sat. and Sun. 9am-6pm, Tel 75420.)

*The bust of Johann Christian Senckenberg, after whom the Museum of Natural History is named*

The museum receives its name from the Frankfurt doctor Johann Christian Senckenberg (1707-1772) who founded the Bürgerhospital and who dreamed of building a "temple of science". But the impetus came from Goethe, at whose urging the Senckenberg Society for the Study of Nature was established in 1817. The society opened a museum in 1821 in the *Eschenheimer Turm*. Collections donated by the African explorer Eduard Rüppel first earned the museum its reputation.

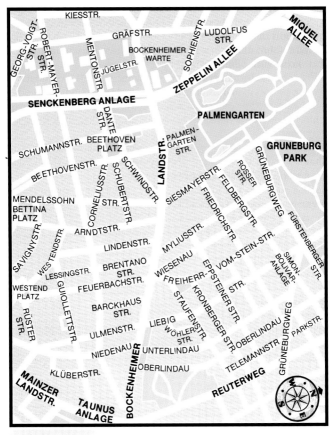

### WESTEND AND BOCKENHEIM

The central building of the present complex on Senckenberganlage, completed in 1907 in baroque style, was designed by Ludwig Neher. The two wings in the same style were added the next year by Franz von Hoven. The right wing houses the museum library, and the left wing, the physics society and observatory. Open arcades link the buildings. Note the figure of *Cronos* with the hourglass and sickle above the pediment.

Senckenberg Museum is best known for its gigantic saurian skeletons. The prehistoric monsters tower two floors – the largest is more than 20 meters (approximately 60 ft.) long and 12 meters (approximately 36 ft.) tall. There are also exhibits of Egyptian animal symbolism, the remains of early Man, of animals, butterflies, and fish from the Main River. There is a display of moon rocks and an environment exhibition. The museum has an Institute of Marine Geology and Biology on the North Sea coast at Wilhelmshaven. There is a restaurant and also a picnic room in the museum.

Senckenberg Museum is adjacent the **Johann Wolfgang Goethe University.** The University was established only in 1914, but the Medical and Science Faculty has its origins much earlier. It was only 18 years after its establishment, in 1932, that the University acquired the name of Johann Wolfgang Goethe University to mark the centenary of Goethe's death.

The University offers a wide range of studies, and is comprised of 21 departments. Due to limited space in the Senckenberganlage, which is the site of the main campus, several university institutes are located elsewhere. The Institute of Nuclear Physics is at the Rebstock Park, while the Institutes of Biology are in the Botanic Gardens. Several other institutes are housed in villas in Westend. Other departments of the University can be found in Niederursel, an outlying area which was incorporated into Frankfurt in 1910. It can be reached by U-3, Niederursel stop.

Throughout the years, the University has prided itself on its high academic level, and several of its lecturers have gained international renown in their fields, such as chemist Paul Ehrlich, sociologist Theodor Adorno and Edinger, the neurologist.

One of Frankfurt's best restaurants, *Humperdinck*, is in the Westend, at 95 Grüneburgweg. Other good restaurants in the quarter include *PX*, at 4 Feldbergstraße, which offers Italian expensive haute cuisine in a glitzy setting. Similarly, you can enjoy pricey Italian haute cuisine with a flair at *Ristorante Incontro*, 64 Kettenhofweg. *Zum Gutenberg*, 22 Savignystraße, is a friendly restaurant that serves large portions of spicy mixed grill dishes upstairs. There is an art gallery downstairs.

*The Observatory at the Senckenberg Museum of Natural History*

# Bockenheim – For a Shopping Break

Bockenheim was once a village which, because of its proximity to the University, had become the city's main student quarter. It can be reached by the U-6 or U-7 to the Bockenheimer Warte or Leipziger Straße stops.

The **Bockenheimer Warte** is one of the late Gothic watchtowers that survived from the town's medieval outer defences. Construction began in 1393, as a solution to the problem of robber knights who were a constant threat to the unprotected town. In 1414, work was begun on replacing the wooden towers with stronger stone towers. The new defensive system took almost 70 years to complete. Its present function is to conceal ventilation shafts of the city's sewers.

*Bockenheimer Warte*

From the Warte, cross to Leipziger Straße to the *Galerie*, a shopping center that includes a good book shop and several good food stores. The restaurant *La Salsicca* is on the back end of the center, and it is a good place for pasta or fresh vegetable concoctions.

Leipziger Straße has maintained its village charm, yet it is one of the more popular

*Bockenheim*

shopping streets in Frankfurt. Take a stroll along it until it ends up in a rather punk neighborhood. If you really feel like hiking, take Konrad-Brosswitzer-Straße and Hedwig-Dransfeld-Straße to the **Women's Peace Church** (Frauen-Friedens-Kirche) at 101 Zeppelinallee. It was built as a memorial to those who died during the First World War. Note the mosaic of the Virgin Mary as a Queen of Peace above the entrance. The stained glass and the Pieta in the crypt are strikingly modern.

*The unique Bockenheimer Warte U-Bahn station*

## Bornheim and the Famous Zoo

Bornheim is another of those villages that managed to retain its character after being swallowed up by Frankfurt. It is the most crowded part of town and its long Berger Straße teems with shoppers. Take the U-4 to Höhenstraße or Bornheim Mitte stops, Bus 32, 34, or 43 or Straßenbahn 12, 23, or 25.

Berger Straße is sometimes called the Bernemer Zeil, but the shops are not as fancy as they are along the Zeil. Walk along the pedestrian precinct (be careful, it is not totally closed to vehicular traffic) past the **Hoher Brunnen** (High Fountain) which was once the source of the public water supply. Philipp Jakob Hoffmann designed the obelisk in 1827. Continue past the Old Town Hall at no. 314, a baroque half-timbered house.

The small square where Berger Straße and Arnsburger Straße meet is the site of a market on Wednesday and Saturday. Notice the clock tower there.

Continue along Berger Straße until it branches, then turn on Alt-Bornheim toward the **St. John's Church** (Johanniskirche). This baroque church with an onion dome was built as parish church in the mid-eighteenth century. It burnt down, but was rebuilt between 1778 and 1781. The half-timbered houses in the surroundings indicate that this was once the village center. In early August the Bornheimer Kerb, a festival primarily for children, takes place here.

At the end of Wittelsbacherallee, at No. 203-205, is the **Church of the Holy Cross** (Heiligkreuzkirche), built between 1928 and 1929 by Martin Weber, and at No. 10 Bornheimer Hang is the Hallgartenschule built between 1929 and 1930. Both are good examples of the period style. The Ernst May housing project of 1926-29 is in this area.

### THE ZOO

To reach the famous **Zoo** (Zoologischer Garten), take U-Bahn 6 or 7 to the Zoo stop, Straßenbahn 18 or Bus 40. Metered streetside parking usually fills up early. Additional parking on Sunday is available at the Großmarkthalle (Wholesale Food Market) on Rückerstraße. The main entrance to the Zoo is on Alfred-Brehm-Platz (named for the eminent naturalist), and there is a second entrance on Röhnstraße. (Open daily at 8am. It closes at 5pm, except for the Exotarium, which is open till 9pm.) The Grzimek House for nocturnal animals opens at 9:30am. The Exotarium can be visited without paying the entire Zoo admission fee. A children's theater is in the main administration building.

Because it is hemmed in by the city, the Zoo is changing its philosophy – moving from big animals to small, from elephants to birds. It is one of the smallest zoos in Europe, but also one of the most respected.

*At the Frankfurt Zoo, whose inhabitants are usually small*

Established in 1858 by Max Schmidt, a veterinary surgeon, it was destroyed by bombs in World War II.

It was rebuilt with the well-being of the animals, as well as the visitors, in mind. Natural enclosures, using water or dry moats as barriers, have replaced cages. Animals that get along well together share enclosures, but they are provided with hiding places.

*Enjoying the cool water*

The Zoo has about 5,000 animals of 600 species, and it is reducing the number of species it has in order to improve the prospects for those it is breeding. For example, the crocodile pit has only one small species, and gives each animal space to stake out its own territory.

A comprehensive 100-page guide book and map in English can be bought at the entrance. It tells about the animals, their eating habits and how they are cared for. Although interesting, it is not really necessary, as each enclosure is labeled with the German, English and scientific name and with a picture of the animal, as well as with a map showing its natural habitat.

One of the best of the Zoo's showcases is the **Grzimek House** (nocturnal animal house), named for the first director of the Zoo after the war. It reverses day and night for the animals so visitors can see them when they are up and about. When new animals for this house are acquired, they must go through a readjustment process much like humans recuperating from jet-lag.

A **Childrens Zoo** is filled with mini-ponies, pygmy goats and pot-bellied pigs. Nearby is a maze, a guinea pig field and the animal nursery.

The **Exotarium** took the place of the

aquarium when the Zoo was rebuilt. It houses not only fish, but also reptiles, arachnids and insects. Its penguins enjoy a polar landscape, while a "tropical storm" takes place twice a day for the jungle animals, reproducing, as far as possible, rain forest conditions.

The Zoo has two restaurants near the entrances, as well as snack bars and ice cream stands.

The Zoo is near the Osthafen (East Harbor), which contains some interesting examples of industrial architecture. It is best viewed from an excursion boat.

## Bergen-Enkheim – A Town with a History

The two communities of Bergen and Enkheim were united in 1936 and were incorporated into Frankfurt only in 1977. The area has a multitude of baroque half-timbered houses. Most of the sites north are in the Bergen section. Take bus 42 or 43 to the **Heimat Museum** (local history museum). (Open Thursday 8am-9:30pm, Sunday 3-6pm.) The museum is in the Old Town Hall on Marktstraße.

The museum has passed through several phases of style: originally Gothic stone in the early fourteenth century, a Renaissance half-timbered superstructure was added between 1520 and 1530, and finally it was enlarged in 1704 in baroque style. It is the perfect place to display the town's cultural development.

Note the **Fratzenstein**, a stone slab built into the west wall (1479) that says in florid script, "Far, du Gauch" (Off, you fool) – a warning to vagrants not to loiter in this town.

At No. 13 Marktstraße is the **Schelmenburg**, a moated mansion standing on the site of a Roman fort. It belonged to the Schelm family, a dynasty of robber knights. After the family died out, their stronghold was demolished and rebuilt in baroque style. It now houses municipal offices.

The **Nikolauskapelle** (St. Nicholas Chapel) stands near the town hall. Built in 1524 for Cistercian monks sent to Bergen to work in the vineyards, it was eventually secularized and is now in poor condition and used for storage. Also part of the abbey property was the *Mönchof* at 95-97 Riedstraße, built between 1771 and 1774.

The town was surrounded by walls in 1440. Of the 10 towers and gates only the 1472 **Weißer Turm** (White Tower) in the Gangstraße survives. Bits of wall can be seen in Im Sperber and Conrad-Weil-Gasse.

Outside town is another tower, the **Berger Warte** (1340), formerly called Geierswarte (Vulture's Tower). Take bus 940 or drive along Vilbeler Landstraße to reach it. It stands out of sight of the road. The tower was destroyed in 1552 in the War of the League of Schmalkalden and rebuilt in 1557. The gallows that stood there were pulled down in 1844, and the stone was used to build the external stairway.

The town festivities are reminiscent of its village days. One of the best is the Open-Air Market in early September, when the cattle are brought to town and the biggest bull wins a prize. There is a parade, and all the accoutrements of a country fair. In October, the town hosts an Applewine Festival.

Bergen-Enkheim elects a Town Scribe every year, a post which has no duties. It pays the writer simply to work creatively.

## Vineyards and Parks – The Greener Side

### Vineyards

The people of Frankfurt have more wine in their cellars than water in their fountains. So went a saying in the Middle Ages.

Today the wine that most people associate with the city is applewine, which is a relative newcomer. But there have been vineyards in and around Frankfurt probably since Roman times, and certainly since the fifteenth century.

The city still has one tiny vineyard, the Lohrberger Hang (Slope). It also owns a large tract at Hochheim am Main, about 20 kilometers away.

The **Lohrberg vineyard** provides more nostalgia than anything else. It is a 1.1 hectare plot of land in the eastern edge of the city – the "door to Germany's Rheingau wine region." Of the country's 11 wine regions, this is considered one of the best.

The Lohrberg vineyard produces about 6,000 liters of wine a year, enough for one bottle per 100 Frankfurters. All the grapes are picked in one day – it takes 50 people about five hours to complete the task. All work in the vineyard is done by hand as it is just too small for machinery.

The Romans brought grape vines to the area when they conquered Germany, and when they left the church took over the vineyards. Wine was an important drink in the Middle Ages since water supplies were often contaminated. The city of Frankfurt, as a commercial center, became the largest wine market in central

Europe. Many Frankfurters have become rich speculating on the wine market.

Vineyards were planted just outside the city walls. First mention of a vineyard was made in 1416, and records show there were vineyards on the Sachsenhäuser Berg, on the Bornheimer Hang, at Fischerfeld, and on the Zeisel on the Friedberger Landstraße. In the nineteenth century the vineyards began to give way to houses and industry. Changes in weather and the destructive vine louse also affected grape growing.

The city acquired the first of its large vineyards at **Hochheim** in 1803, during the Napoleonic invasions when the churches were forced to rid themselves of their large holdings. The vineyard was enlarged after World War II.

Currently the Hochheim vineyard produces 100,000 to 270,000 liters of wine per year, depending on the weather. City vintners boast of the high quality wine Hochheim produces, mainly because the climate and soil are ideal, as a result of being warmed by winds from North Africa.

To visit the Lohrberg vineyard, drive along Friedberger Landstraße (Highway 3) toward Bad Vilbel to the Heiligenstock (signs will direct you to the vineyard), or take Bus 38 or 69. It is about half an hour's walk from the bus stop to the vineyard, past rows of tiny garden plots that Frankfurters rent.

The vineyard is on the slope facing the city, offering a marvelous view on a clear day. Behind it is a large park that has a terrace restaurant. The food is served in large portions and is inexpensive, but not particularly good.

It is possible to visit the wine estate at **Hochheim**, as well. Visits to the vineyard and tastings from the barrels can be arranged for groups of 20 to 30 people. Offices for information and reservations are at 11 Aichgasse. Open 8am-noon.

Frankfurt wine is sold at the Stadt Weingut in the Römer, 2 Limpurgergasse, from 7:30am-4pm. Lohrberger wine is sold in a six-pack mix with two other Frankfurt wines. Its label bears a picture of medieval Frankfurt and the portraits of two of the city's favorite writers, Goethe and the dialect writer Friedrich Stoltze (1816-1891).

## Parks

Frankfurt has quite a lot of green space, of which its citizens are very fond. They often stroll in the parks, even when the weather requires boots and umbrellas. The route begins with the larger and better known parks and then briefly look at some of the lovely small areas of greenery.

### THE PALMENGARTEN

The Palmengarten (Palm Garden) is a popular playground and recreation spot for young and old alike. There are paddle boats, tennis courts, and mini-golf. Outdoor concerts take often place here.

*Weird creatures and lots of flowers at the Palmengarten*

The main entrance is at the end of Palmengartenstraße, reached via Bockenheimer Landstraße from U-Bahn stops at Westend or Bochenheimer Warte. Another entrance is at 61 Siesmayerstraße, near the U.S. Consulate, reached by Bus 36. A third entrance is on Zeppelinallee, reached by Bus 32. Gardens open daily at 9am in winter and close between 4pm in winter and 6pm in summer. The buildings are closed about one

*A greenhouse in the Palmengarten*

hour before the gardens are closed, except for special events held in the buildings.

The gardens and the greenhouses are the main attraction of the Palmengarten. It was established in 1869 when a collection of plants were purchased from Duke Adolf of Nassau. The plants came from the huge park of Biebrich Castle, which lies on the Rhine River at Wiesbaden.

Heinrich Siesmayer landscaped the gardens from between 1872 and 1874, and they have been extended three times since then. The area includes many theme gardens, a large collection of cacti and tropical plants, and an Alpine Garden. In the summer, stroll through the gardens and meadow or relax in a terrace café. In the winter, you might choose to take refuge in the hot-houses or visit one of the exhibitions that are mounted almost monthly.

The assembly hall, where private social events can be held, is the work of revolutionary architect Ernst May, who, with Martin Elsässer, reconstructed the building in 1929.

Two of the biggest events held in the Palmengarten are the Rose Show in June and the Festival of Lights with fireworks, which takes place in August. The *Palmenrestaurant* is good and there are fast-food stands as well.

On the northern edge of the gardens is the *Villa Leonhardsbrunn*, built in 1840 but recently renovated. It serves as a school for florists and gardeners.

The Palmengarten adjoins the huge Grüneburg Park.

## GRÜNEBURG PARK

Grüneburg Park takes its name from the fourteenth-century fortified manor that stood here. It was rebuilt in 1837, from which time it was owned by Meyer Amschel Rothschild, patriarch of the banking family. He had the park landscaped in English style. Heinrich Siesmayer, who designed the Palmengarten, redesigned Grüneburg Park between 1880 and 1903.

The garden contains a small porter's lodge from about 1875 and, opposite it, an octagonal pavilion from Bockenheim. In the south east corner of the park is the heavily-fenced I.G. Farben Building, sometimes simply called the **Hochhaus**. It was among the few buildings not damaged in the air raid of March 1944. It has been turned into headquarters for the U.S. Army's Fifth Corps, though it has been the property of the Federal Government since 1955.

The building, with its white travertine facade, is a fine example of functional architecture. It was built between 1928 and 1930 for the huge I.G. Farben Chemical Corporation on the site of a hospital for the insane. Heinrich Hoffmann, the famous nineteenth-century doctor and writer, was once the director of this hospital.

*Art among the lush greenery*

## THE STADTWALD

The Stadtwald (City Forest) is a huge area of greenery along the southern side of the city. It belongs to Sachsenhausen and stretches almost 16 kilometers from Kelsterbach in the west, to Offenbach in the east. It has many paths for walking, horseback riding, and cycling, and even though the area includes the noisy airport and is cut through by expressways, there is space enough for seclusion. It includes the Waldstadion (the forest's football stadium), a golf course and a playground (at the junction of Niederräder Landstraße and Mörfelder Landstraße).

Frankfurt's *Wäldchesta*g holiday is a forest celebration. It takes place the Tuesday after Withsun (Pentecost), primarily in the vicinity of the **Oberforsthaus** (Forester's House) at Niederrad, which can be reached by Mörfelder Landstraße, Bus 61, or Straßenbahn 15. Carnival rides and booths are set up for the festivities. Shops and offices close for the afternoon, and the townsfolk come out to revel in the greenery.

A pleasant forest outing is to the **Oberschweinstiege**, so named because pigs were once driven into the forest to feed on the acorns there. (There is also an Unterschweinstiege near the airport.) The Oberschweinstiege can be reached by car from the Darmstädter Landstraße or by Straßenbahn 14. There is a horse corral for those who ride.

*The Stadtwald – the countryside within the city*

An outdoor terrace restaurant, which specializes in German dishes is situated on a

peninsula that juts into the Jaco-biweiher, a large artificial pond. Paths lead around the pond, which attracts a variety of water-fowl.

Another good starting point for a walk through the forest is the **Goethe Tower** (Goether Turm) on the eastern side of the forest. It can be reached by the Baben-häuser Landstraße or by Bus 36 or 960. It is the tallest wooden tower in Germany at 44 meters (approximately 130 feet), and was made in 1931 from forest timber. Climb it for a good view of the city. There is a playground for children here, as well as a restaurant.

*Climb the Goethe Tower for a good view of the city*

Farther out Babenhäuser Land-straße is Monte Scherbelino, a hill built between 1927 and 1928 out of 20 million tons of rubble – the city dump. After a new refuse plant was set up, the hill was landscaped and turned into a playground. There are picnic tables, a toboggan run and a pond at the foot of the hill.

## THE WALLANLAGEN

The Wallanlagen (City Ring) is a crescent of narrow promenades following the old city ramparts. The walls were torn down in the nineteenth century, and the promenades were laid out during the period that Jakob Guiollett served as mayor. Like many of Frankfurt's patrician families, the Guiolletts were of French Huguenot descent. Sebastian Rinz, the city gardener, was the landscape artist.

The **Gallusanlage** sits behind the Municipal Theater, where the western end of the ring meets the Main River. Here you can see one of Frankfurt's prettiest fountains, the

**Märchenbrunnen** (Fairy-Tale Fountain), which dates from 1910. The model for the central figure is said to have been a young laundress. The bronze figures of fish and children that once adorned the rims disappeared during World War II.

Following the ring across Kaiserstraße into the **Taunusanlage**, and you will approach several monuments to great Germans. The first is a larger-than-life **statue of Goethe**, moved from the Goetheplatz after the war. Characters from his works appear on three sides of the base, and in the front are the figures Science, Drama and Poetry. The statue, by Ludwig von Schwanthalen, dates from 1840.

Next comes the Opfern, a monument (Benno Elkan, 1920) dedicated to those who fell during World War I. The Schiller Monument (Dielmann, 1864) stands at Große Gallusstraße, the Heine Monument (Georg Kolbe, 1913) is in the middle of this section, and the **Beethoven Monument** (designed by Kolbe in 1926, but cast 1948) stands near Junghofstraße. At the corner of Mainzer Landstraße is a small fountain called Lachhannes (Laughing Hans), which depicts a grape picker (Johann Nepomuk Zwerger, 1859).

Nearer the Opera House is the Guiollett Monument, which honors the mayor who established the parks. Banks now dominate this area.

Continue across the Operplatz. Behind the Opera House, the parks begin again, this time **Bockenheimer Anlage**, one of the loveliest sections of the ring, which was relandscaped in 1981.

There is a large fish pond and an indoor public pool – Stadtbad Mitte - and between the two stands the **Nebbiensches Garten-haus** (Nebbien Garden-House), built by Danish publisher Markus Johann Nebbien. Note the sixteenth century Italian well that stands beside the house.

At the end of this section of park is the **Schwindhaus**, a neoclassical villa built in 1845 for the painter Moritz von Schwind. You will approach, once again, the Eschen-heimer Turm at its busy intersection. The complex of fountains here, built in 1970, were designed by Hermann Goepfert.

It is just a few steps back into the peaceful green space of the **Eschenheimer Anlage**. The monument to Philipp Reis, who developed a telephone in 1861, is near the intersection. The Bürgergarten near the Löwenstein Palais contains a Medusa Fountain. Many late-neoclassical houses stand along the side streets. The bronze bust is of Anton Kirchner (1779-1835), the first man to write a complete history of Frankfurt. The bust is by Heinrich Petry, 1879.

*The park is an ideal place for a peaceful stroll with the children*

At the intersection of Friedberger Landstraße and Friedberger Anlage is **Bethmanns Park**, named for the Frankfurt banker and philanthropist Simon Moritz von Bethmann and added to the ring of parks in 1952. The Hessian Monument, dating from 1794, was a gift to the city from King Frederick William of Prussia.

The *Odeon*, now a café but built in 1815 as a museum in honor of Bethmann, offers an attractive view from its terrace. The small pond is the Bethmannweiher. Nearby is a bust of Bethmann by Eduard Schmidt von der Launitz (1868).

You are now in **Friedberger Anlage**, sliced in two by the Zeil. A stone at the south side

*A quiet walk, accompanied by some of the park's feathered residents*

of the Zeil marks the site of a synagogue destroyed by the Nazis in 1938. The Rinz memorial honors Sebastian Rinz, the city gardener who created the Wallanlage. This section of the ring ends at Allerheiligentor (All Saints' Gate).

The **Obermainanlage** has a large pond called Rechneigrabenweiher, near a home for senior citizens. Here you can see a bronze bust of Schopenhauer, by Friedrich Schierholz dating from 1895, and a marble bust of the eighteenth-century author Gotthold Ephraim Lessing.

Near the end of the ring stands the **Holy Ghost Hospital** (Hospital zum Heiligen Geist), a neoclassical structure built between 1835 and 1839. A few fragments of the old town wall remain in the upper gardens.

### GÜNTHERSBURG PARK
This park in Bornheim, is bordered on the front by schools and at the back by the city *Gärtnerei* (nursery). It can be reached by Straßenbahn 12 or 25, Bus 34, 38 or 69. A Roman villa from the second century has been excavated at the western end. The noble family Weiß von Limpurg had a moated manor here during the Middle Ages, but the house burnt down in 1552. Later, the Imperial War Commissioner Johann Jacob Günther built a mansion known as the Günthersburg. The Rothschild family purchased the estate in 1832, and in 1892 it was opened as a Volkspark (People's Park). There are some lovely old trees here, and a fountain that is ideal for children, who can play in it.

### HOLZHAUSEN PARK
A moated manor house, the Holzhausenschlößchen, stands on the Justinianstraße edge of this park. It can be reached by U-1,

2, or 3 and Bus 36. The Family von Holzhausen owned the property from 1503 until 1910. Their first country mansion burnt down in the mid-sixteenth century during the War of the League of Schmalkalden. It was rebuilt as a fortified manor and survived the Thirty Years' War. Between 1726 and 1729, it was redesigned by Louis Remy de la Fosse, architect of the Landgrave of Hessen, as a country estate.

### ROTHSCHILD PARK

The Rothschild Park, where Bockenheimer Landstraße and Bockenheimer Anlage meet, is most notable for its ring of statues by Georg Kolbe. The bronze figures, set between pillars, are *Young Wife*, *Herd Girl*, *The Chosen One* and *Amazon*, all designed between 1939 and 1941. *Standing Youth*, *Thinker* and *Man Walking Downhill* date from between 1945 and 1948.

The **Amerikahaus**, a cultural center that promotes German-American relations, stands at one end of the park on Reuterweg.

### THE REBSTOCK PARK

Located beyond the Messe at August-Euler-Straße, the Rebstock is used as a parking lot during large fairs, during which time there is shuttle bus service to the fair. It can be reached by Bus 33 or 34.

This was Frankfurt's first airport, and served as a landing field for Zeppelins. A stone carved by Martin Elsässer stands as a memorial to the first aircraft landing there.

The **Rebstockbad**, which opened in 1982, is a swimming and recreation center. It includes a warm-water pool with a wave machine, a heated outdoor pool, and a pool for the handicapped. It also contains a gym, solarium, saunas, cafés, a restaurant, and conference rooms.

## Cemeteries

We have included some of the more interesting cemeteries which are lovely oases of green, and because they provide an interesting way to learn about the city's culture and history.

### THE OLD JEWISH CEMETERY

The oldest Jewish Cemetery in Frankfurt, which was in use from 1462 to 1825, is on Batton Straße not far from the Allerheiligentor. It can be reached by Straßenbahn 11 or 14. To visit, you must make arrangements with the Jewish Community Administration, (Tel. 740721), or take one of the walking tours occasionally scheduled by the city historical society. The cemetery is near the ghetto, where the Jews were forced to live from 1460 until 1811.

### HAUPTFRIEDHOF

The Hauptfriedhof (Main Cemetery) lies between Eckenheimer Landstraße and Friedberger Landstraße above Nibelungenallee. It can be reached by the U-5, Straßenbahn 25, or Bus 32 or 34.

Opened outside town in 1828 to replace the Petersfriedhof, it contains the graves of some of Frankfurt's best-known citizens. Among them are members of the Bethmann banking family, philosophers Theodor W. Adorno (1903-1969) and Arthur Schopenhauer (1788-1860), doctor and creator of *Struwwelpeter* Heinrich Hoffmann (1809-1894), anthropologist Leo Frobenius (1873-1938), architect Ernst May (1886-1970), and spokesman for the Young Germany Movement Carl Ferdinand Gutzkow (1811-1878). There is a monument to the victims of the Holocaust.

The late-classical Altes Portal near the corner of Eckenheimer and Nibelungen was designed by the city architect Friedrich Rumpf. Behind it stretches a line of 52 arcades, beautifully set off by an English garden landscaped by Sebastian Rinz, the man responsible for the Wallanlagen parks.

As the cemetery was expanded at the turn of the century, a Neues Portal (New Gate) was built, along with a mortuary and crematorium. An old Jewish cemetery lies in the south eastern corner and a new Jewish cemetery in the northwestern corner.

### THE PETERSFRIEDHOF

The Petersfriedhof (St. Peter's Cemetery) was once the main cemetery of Frankfurt. Used as a burial place since 1419, many of Frankfurt's patrician families are buried here: Cronstetten, Glauburg, Holzhausen, Hynsperg, Knoblauch, Limpurg, Melem. The tombstone of Goethe's father, who died in 1782, is on the western wall. The crucifixion is a copy of the work by Hans Backoffen (the original is in the Historical Museum).

# OUTLYING AREAS

In the near neighborhood of Frankfurt are some lovely and interesting areas. Höchst, which gave its name to a giant chemical concern, became part of Frankfurt in 1928, but lies at some distance from the center of town. Offenbach, in the opposite direction, grew up as the center of Germany's leather industry, and is the site of several international leather fairs and fashion shows, as well as home of the German Leather Museum. Hanau, to the east, has two castles, a Doll Museum and a Gold and Silversmith's Museum. To the north is Bad Nauheim, a spa with some of the loveliest Jugendstil (art nouveau) buildings to be found anywhere. Elvis Presley fans will recognize this as the place "The King" spent his stint in the Army.

## Höchst – Medieval and Modern

Höchst is situated on the banks of the Main where the Nidda River joins it, about 10 kilometers from the middle of Frankfurt. It can be reached by the S-Bahn-1 or S-2, or (for the best view) by ferry from Höchsterweg. It was a trading settlement in Roman times, and the Romans had a brick kiln here. In 1355 it was presented its charter by Emperor Charles IV. Höchst was used by the Prince Bishops of Mainz in their struggles against the Free Imperial City of Frankfurt. It was plundered during the Thirty Years' War and its castle was almost totally destroyed. During the eighteenth century, industries were established here.

In spite of industrial development, the town retains its character and it has the only preserved medieval town square in Frankfurt. In an ongoing tradition that has lasted 600 years, a market takes place here each Tuesday, Friday, and Saturday. Many of the half-timbered houses surrounding the square have been restored.

Each summer Höchst hosts a Castle Festival (Schloß Fest) and the Jazz-Festival-on-the-Burggraben, the street that follows the old castle moat.

It is best to approach Höchst by the ferry from Schwanheim. It runs irregularly – whenever there are enough passengers, from morning until dark for both cars and pedestrians. From the ferry, there is a view of the remains of the city walls, as well as of the Castle and the Church of St. Justin. Disembark on the Batterie and walk over to the Castle.

**Höchst Castle** (Höchster Schloß) stands in the Schloßplatz surrounded by several quaint houses. Over the centuries, several forts and castles have stood here. A moated castle was built on the site in the fourteenth century. The present Renaissance castle is part of a complex constructed between 1586 and 1608, incorporating the already-standing Customs Tower (Zollturm) and the old palace tower. Even after the castle was destroyed in 1635, the towers remained. Two museums are housed in the restored castles – the **Museum of the History of Höchst** and the **Museum of Höchst AG**. (Open daily 10am-4pm.)

Walk along the Burggraben until it turns onto Bolongarostraße. Just inside the town walls stands the **Dalberghaus**, which houses the porcelain factory. The house has a vaulted cellar and a half-timbered top floor. It was built in 1582 and rebuilt immediately after the great fire of 1586.

*The wonderfully preserved towers of Höchst Castle*

The porcelain factory built in 1746 was the third to be established in Europe, preceded by the factories built in Dresden in 1711 and Vienna in 1719. Today it produces mainly copies of eighteenth-century designs, especially those of Laurentius Russinger (1753-67) and Johann Peter Melchior (1768-79). The rose-lavender glaze is unique to Höchst porcelain.

Further along Bolongarostraße is the **Cronberger Haus**, a stone house which was built between 1577 and 1580, but whose present architecture dates from the nineteenth century. It stands opposite the remains of the

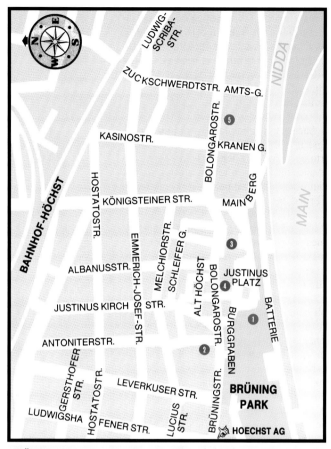

## HÖCHST

1. Schloß Höchst
2. Dalberghaus
3. Antoniterkloster
4. Altes Rathaus
5. Bolongaropalast

**Antonite Friary** (Antoniterkloster) at 139-43 Bolongarostraße. The Antonites were a secular order, and this was their largest house in Germany. Note the stucco ceiling on the upper floor. The northern wing of the building, with a Late Gothic gable, survived the demolition of 1809-1811, when most of the other structures were torn down.

Continue for some distance along Bolongarostraße to the **Bolongaro Palace**

(Bolongaropalast), a huge building owned by the town and used for administrative offices. (Open weekdays 9am-4pm, Sun. 10am-noon.) It was built between 1772 and 1774 by the Bolongaro brothers, Josef Maria Markus and Jakob Philipp, who came here from Italy.

The baroque palace fans out into three wings. Its gardens are laid out in terraces overlooking the confluence of the Nidda and the Main. Weddings often take place in the Wedding Room of the palace on Wednesday and Friday mornings.

The old **snuff factory** stands next door on Kranengasse. It was built at the same time as the palace, but in a simpler style. It ceased to operate in 1785, shortly after the deaths of the Bolongaro brothers.

Stroll back along the Main to the Justinus-platz to visit **St. Justin's Church** (Justinus-Kirche), which is perched high above the town walls. This was one of the first churches to be built in Germany and is the oldest in Frankfurt. It dates from the ninth century, when the relics of St. Justin were brought here, but has undergone much renovation since then. The long Carolingian nave with its fine columned arches has survived. Notice the leaf-capitals of the columns. The figures of St. Paul of Thebes and St. Antony the Hermit that fan the main doorway are copies – the originals are inside.

Between the church and the castle you will see the **Old Town Hall** (Altes Rathaus), its step-gables topped by stone balls. It was built after the fire of 1586 by the Italian architect Oswald Stupanus.

Two other points of interest in Höchst are **Höchst AG** and the Jahrhunderthalle. Established in 1863, as a dye manufacturer, Farbwerke Meister, Lucius & Brünning, Höchst AG is one of the world's largest producers of medicines, dyes and synthetic

fibers today. The factory lies on the Main between Höchst and Sindlingen. The administrative offices at the end of Brüningstraße (an extension of Bolongarostraße) are a fine example of Expressionist architecture. Built in between 1920 and 1924 by Peter Behrens, they consist of two unequal sections of clinker brick that intersect at an angle. Pillars rise from the entry hall, growing closer together at the top. Light comes through the cupolas in the roof, and the colors graduate from warm at the bottom to cool at the top. The bridge from these offices to the old building (1893) was also designed by Behrens and has been taken as symbol for the company. Visits can be arranged by appointment. Tel. 305-6666.

The firm marked its 100th birthday in 1963 by the building **Jahrhunderthalle Höchst** (Höchst Century Hall). It is at 301 Pfaffenwiese on the road to Zeilsheim. You cannot miss the concrete dome with a diameter of 86 meters (282 feet). It is a popular cultural center for Frankfurt: opera, rock concerts, theater and ballet performances are held here. There is also an hotel in the complex, as well as a casino and restaurant.

## Offenbach – The Leather Center

Offenbach lies on the Main just southeast of the Frankfurt city center, a direct drive from Sachsenhausen along the Deutschherrnufer or the Offenbacher Landstraße. It can be reached by S-8 or Straßenbahn 16. It is a lively town in its own right, owing a great deal to its large foreign population. It has a good flea market Saturday mornings on the river near the Carl-Ulrich-Brucke.

Of the 26,000 people working in Germany's leather industry, one-third are in Offenbach. The industry got its start in the early

nineteenth century with the manufacture of small cases and portfo-
lios, and Offenbach soon developed a reputation for producing
high-quality articles. It received another boost when the handbag
became popular during the women's emancipation movement.

The **Printing and Graphics Museum**
(Klingspor-Museum) at 80 Herrnstraße has
an international collection of modern book
designs and poster illustrations. Its **Bunte
Kinderwelt** (Children's World in Color)
exhibition shows the latest children's books
from all over the world. (Open daily 10am-
5pm. Closed for lunch 1-2pm Sat. and Sun.)

The **City Museum** (Stadtmuseum), at 80
Parkstraße, has a good collection of Offenbach pottery, for which the town gained
fame in the eighteenth century. (Open Tues.-
Sun. 10am-5pm, Wed. 2-8pm.)

Twice a year Offenbach hosts a fashion
preview of small leather goods and twice a
year, coinciding with the Frankfurt Fair, the
International Leathergoods Fair takes place
there. The shows are not open to the public,
so to see something of leather, go to the
Leather Museum.

The **German Leather Museum** (Deutsches
Ledermuseum), at 86 Frankfurter Straße,
was founded in 1917. (Open daily 10am-
5pm. Group tours in English can be
arranged.) The museum originally served as
a showcase of leather fashions, at a time
when people were deploring "poor design"
and were upholding the eighteenth and nineteenth centuries as standards of excellence.
Now, however, it tries to show the importance of leather in certain cultures of the
world. It covers the techniques of working
leather and has a large collection of leather
objects. It has a separate **Shoe Museum**
(Deutsche Schuhmuseum).

The excellent American Indian section is
very popular with the Germans who have
romantic ideas about the Wild West. The
African section focuses on herding tribes of

the west. There are also sections devoted to Asia and Mexico.

The best place in town to eat is the *Datscha*, a Russian restaurant in the small, attractive *Hotel Kaiserhof*, 8a Kaiserstraße. Tel. 885581 (restaurant). Tel. 814054 (hotel). The restaurant is open only in the evenings and is moderately priced. It is a stone's throw from the railway station. Although the neighborhood is a bit down-at-the-heel at this end of the street, it has convenient access to public transport and the center of town.

For information about Offenbach, contact the Tourist Information Office, 17 Stadthof, Tel. 80652946.

## Hanau – Silver, Gold and Castles

Hanau is the birthplace of the Brothers Grimm, and it is the starting point of the German Fairy Tale Road that goes north all the way to Bremen. The town itself was almost wiped out in World War II, so you will have to search for the treasures that remain. You can reach Hanau by Autobahn SS or the S-7.

The **Deutsches Goldschmiedehaus** (German Goldsmith's House) stands at Altstödter Markt, on the old market square. Do not confuse this with the new market at the Town Hall in the pedestrian zone, a bit to the south.

The house is half-timbered, dating from the sixteenth century. A stone well chiseled in 1611 complements the house. It served as a town hall, storage place, and girls school before a goldsmith named Ferdinand Wilm suggested that it be used as exhibition space for Hanau craftsmen. Jewelry and precious metals have long played an important role in Hanau's economy. Still today, many jewelers learn their trade here. In 1772, a Public Academy of Drawing was established by the smiths, and continues to attract students from all over Europe. (Open Tues.-Sun. 10-12am, 2-5pm).

**Philipp's Rest Castle** (Schloß Philippsruhe) is in Kesselstadt, just to the west of Hanau, directly on the bank of the Main. (Open daily, except Monday, 10am-5pm.) It can be reached by driving from Hanau along Philippsruherallee or from the Hanau-West railway station. The castle is backed by a landscaped park and a footpath running beside the Main. Sometimes you can see a shepherd grazing his sheep here.

The castle was built for Count Philipp Reinhard in 1701. The top floor was destroyed by fire, but restoration was completed in 1987. The museum sells a fascinating book of photographs of the fire.

The castle entrance is airy. Note the repetition of the lion motif on the door handles. Climb up the grand staircase. Upstairs you are required to place grey felt slippers over your shoes to protect the exquisite parquet floors – each room in a different pattern. The walls are wood panneled, as well, and the old porcelain stoves are exquisite. Take note of the splendid ceiling decorations.

There is a restaurant with terrace in the riverside wing of the castle, but many people prefer to picnic along the Main.

**Wilhelmsbad**, a former spa whose Cure House (*Kurhaus*) still stands, is just to the north of the castle and can be reached from Burgallee. The English-style park is open all year round. It stretches out in front of the elegant spa complex, which was built in 1779 by Crown-Prince Wilhelm of Hesse-Kassel. A modern-art gallery, theather (*Komödienhaus*), and restaurant are now housed in the buildings. The "ruin" that stands on an island in the nearby pond was put there when the park was laid out. The little pyramid is the tomb of Wilhelm's young son. Wander along the footpaths until you find the old carousel. It is no longer in use and is a bit weathered, but the elegant carriages and wooden horses are still delightful.

In another part of the park is the **Doll Museum** (Puppenmuseum), a golf course, and the small, attractive *Golf Hotel* at Wilhelmsbaderallee, Tel. 06181-83219.

For more information about Hanau, contact the Tourist Information Office, Tel. 06181-252400.

## Bad Nauheim – Bathing in Jugendstil

Jugendstil is the German term for that short-lived but exciting style in art and architecture, at the turn of the century, usually known as Art Nouveau. This style first developed in Germany at Darmstadt (about 25 kilometers south of Frankfurt) at the artists' colony around the Mathildenhöhe. Some examples survive there, but for the largest complex of Jugendstil buildings in the country, head north to Bad Nauheim. It is north of Frankfurt and can be reached by Autobahn 5, or the S-6 to Friedberg and a bus from there.

The little town is still a spa (the name *Bad* in German means bath) and its Jugendstil spa center extends from the railway station to the Cure Park (*Kurpark*). You cannot miss the copper-domed buildings as you approach from the railway station.

Bad Nauheim has been an enclave of the rich and famous since these elaborate bathing facilities were installed. It began as a treatment center for employees of its salt works. Among the elite visitors was U.S. President, Franklin D. Roosevelt. He spent a couple of years there as a child, and many local people believe that is why the town was spared bombing in World War II, even though a Nazi radio transmitter was set up there.

When the war was over, Bad Nauheim served as the headquarters for the U.S. Army before they were moved to Heidelberg. This is where Elvis Presley was stationed when he was in the Army, and every year an "Elvis Reunion" is held in the new *Kurhaus*.

Since the war, the nature of the spa business has changed. Many private clinics have access to the warm mineral springs underneath the town, which means that some spa buildings are not in use. Visitors must take a guided tour to them. Tours are given year-round on Wednesday at 3pm in German, but English tours can be arranged for groups. In addition, the guides of the German tour usually speak English. The tours begin underneath the fountains in the center of the complex.

Three wells produce water with a salt content equal to that of the North Sea and with a temperature of 86°F (30°C). A section of clear tubing shows the water flowing through the pipes. The water does not have to be pumped because of the natural pressure.

The water, which comes from an ancient volcano in the Vogelsberg, is high in carbon dioxide, so when it reaches the open air, rust forms quickly. The water bubbles out white from the fountains, but the pools are a murky red.

Schematic diagrams on the walls underneath the fountain show the geological split (limestone and quartz collide and force the water to the surface) that has blessed the town with the healing water. Another drawing shows how the mineral's strength can be regulated for various treatments.

The center of the complex is the **Sprudelhof** (Fountain Court), built between 1905 and 1911. The complex is best known for its stained-glass windows. The windows in the administration building at 20 Ludwigstraße provide a fine example.

The courtyard at Bath House is also renowned. It is surrounded by the building arcades held by stylized-figure columns in Italian terra cotta, designed in Darmstadt. The courtyard is perfectly quiet, and it is very inviting to relax on the terra cotta benches, amid flowers spilling red, blue, purple, yellow over the gravel path. The figures on the columns are mainly water creatures. The appreciation of water and health is symbolized throughout the complex.

Though the bath houses appear to be the same at first glance, a peek inside reveals that the decorations differ from one to the next. Each has a waiting room done in

*Health and pleasure combine in the spa treatment center*

ceramics, mosaics, or marble, with finely-crafted copper camouflage for the radiators.

Radiator heat was an advanced notion for the times, and was installed because it was much healthier for the patients than breathing sooty air. The heating plant, whose chimney soars behind the railway station, still provides warmth for the spa as well as for the U.S. Army facilities in town.

The individual treatment cabins in the bath houses also differ decoratively and many still have their oversized hospital-white chairs. The tubs are wooden and a row of knobs along the fronts control the various types of water treatment. Each tub has a built-in towel-warming compartment. When a patient finishes the bath, he is wrapped in warm towels and allowed to rest.

Once the spa had four special baths for royalty, but now only one is open – patronized exclusively by a Saudi man who has been using the facilities for more than 20 years. His bath is all marble, with brass fittings and gold-plated mosaics, but the decor is more classical than typical Jugendstil.

The bathing treatments are given in the **Sprudelhof**. A second treatment center is the **Trinkkuranlage** (Drink Center). This facility is set apart from the other buildings, beyond a church that stands on the site of the town's first spa.

The Trinkanlage is also in Jugendstil, and is set in a park where the town orchestra plays in the bandshell beside the pool on sunny afternoons. Inside the hall, one can rent a handled glass of pink, green, or clear crystal, marked in milliliter measures, and taste the water.

The octagonal water bar is decorated with brown and green ceramics from the Darmstadt school. The patient drinks from one of three wells, each of which has its own set of brass spigots, and water can be ordered warm or cold. It tastes better cold, but is healthier when warm – and it really does taste medicinal.

Water from the Karl's Fountain (Karlsbrunnen) is good for the stomach and contains one percent salt; water from the Kurbrunnen (Cure Fountain) is good for the liver and contains 1.2 percent salt. Heart and kidney patients get the best-tasting water (although it smells of sulphur) that comes from the Ludwigsbrunnen, containing 0.1 percent salt.

Health care is centered at these two areas, but the town's cultural and social center is the **Kurhaus**. Set behind a bank of flowers at the end of the manicured Kurpark, the sprawling building contains meeting and party rooms of all sizes, a café, a good but expensive restaurant, and the luxurious *Parkhotel*, belonging to the Best Western chain. The Theater is also found here. It was destroyed in a fire, but was rebuilt in its original style. In the foyer are seven Jugendstil paintings from Bath House 2.

A horse-and-carriage tour of the town operates year-round, provided you can locate the driver near the Trinkkuranlage. The town is at its most festive on the last Sunday in August, when the fountains are turned on full blast, the town swings to the rhythm of brass bands, and the day comes to a close with fireworks.

For information contact the Kurverwaltung, Neue Kolonnade an der Dankeskirche, 6350 Bad Nauheim, Tel. 06032-2120, fax 06032-35142.

# DAY TRIPS

Frankfurt is an ideal base for day trips. It is surrounded by a number of cities important in their own right, and is within day-trip reach of such places as Heidelberg, with its famous castle ruin; Rothenburg o.d. Tauber, a walled city that clings to its medieval character; and Strasbourg, France, worth a visit for the food and the Cathedral. It is an easy drive to the Alsace region of France for lunch in one of the superb restaurants there.

However, we will present four interesting day trips very nearby, so that you spend minimum time on the road and maximum time enjoying your experiences. You will visit two neighboring cities, Wiesbaden and Mainz, then tour the Taunus Range, and finally take a cruise up the Rhine River, stopping at Rüdesheim.

## Wiesbaden

The German synonym for elegance is Wiesbaden. You have only to walk along the Wilhelmstraße, known to the locals simply as "The Rue," to pause in the tree-shaded Warmer Damm park or look in on the gilt and crystal casino in order to feel the charm of the city.

Not that the city does not have a lively side, too. The Rhein-Main Halle is the venue for big pop concerts, and jazz clubs appear frequently. The Kurhaus, the city's social center, even stages American country music shows. Festivals take place year-round: the Rheingau Wine Fest in August, the Christmas Market in December, and the May Festival which attracts the best international music ensembles.

Wiesbaden is also the capital of the German state of Hesse, which has a population of about 250,000. Parliament convenes in the white palace of the Dukes of Nassau at the market square.

Linked by Autobahn 66, and by the S-1 or S-14, Wiesbaden is about 36 kilometers from Frankfurt. In summer, excursion boats ply the river between the cities.

Wiesbaden owes much of its character to its cold and hot water thermal springs. In the middle of the 19th century it became the summer residence of the German emperors, and most of the inner city was built then.

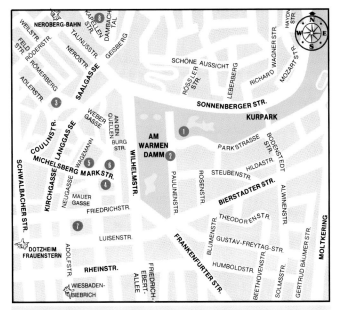

### WIESBADEN

1. Kurhaus
2. Hessen State Theater
3. Kaiser-Friedrich Bad
4. Rathaus
5. Landtag
6. Marktkirche
7. St. Bonifatius
8. Greek Chapel

The late-Classical style, typical of the city, adds to its charm.

Wiesbaden has always attracted the wealthy. You can see them along the Wilhelmstraße, shopping in the exclusive stores or relaxing at the *Park Café*. It is a wonderful street for shopping or window-shopping – start at the corner of Friedrichstraße – or stroll along the other side of the street through the Warmer Damm.

This will take you to the **Hessen State Theater**, which overlooks a pair of three-tiered fountains to the Brunnenkolonnade (Fountain Colonnade), which is a stretch of white pillars with benches for relaxing.

The **Kurhaus** (casino) in the left wing and

the meeting center and concert hall in the right complete the building complex.

The 40-million-mark renovation of the Kurhaus was completed in December 1987. The main concert hall was restored exactly like the original. Among the smaller salons are the Mussel Room, its pillars made of gravel and topped with seashells, and a Dostoyevsky Room, named in honor of the famous Russian writer who gambled at the casino here.

The casino has an international section with Black Jack and Roulette, and a small section with slot machines. A corner of the main gambling hall has been converted into a restaurant, which is an exciting place to have a meal, and the food is good. A screen shows what is happening at the gaming tables every 30 seconds, and diners can watch as the gamblers dash away to try their luck. The restaurant is closed Monday; reservations are advisable, especially on weekends.

The *Bistro*, outside the gambling area, is a pleasant place for a less-expensive (though certainly not cheap) meal. It has a piano bar. The casino provides shuttle bus service from Frankfurt.

Behind the Kurhaus is the beautifully manicured Kurpark. On the Wilhelmstraße facing the Kurhaus is the *Nassauer Hof*, the most luxurious hotel in town, with a superb restaurant, *Die Ente von Lehel*. It is regarded as one of the best restaurants in Germany.

Continue to stroll along Wilhelmstraße to the Kranzplatz. As you approach this square, you can see the steam rising from the Kochbrunnen, the city's favorite hot spring. Its water bubbles up from a depth of 2,000 meters (over 5,000 feet), and reaches 154°F (67°C). A four-spigoted fountain protected by a small "temple" is there for anyone who wants to sip the curative mineral water. Some people carry collapsible cups with them for this purpose. Some buildings nearby are heated with the thermal water, but mineral deposits create a problem with the plumbing.

You may walk up Taunusstraße to browse in the antique shops or duck into the "Bermuda Triangle" (so named because you can get lost there) at Nerostraße, which is packed full of bars and jazz clubs. You can also go to the **Kaiser-Friedrich Bad** at 38-40 Langgasse where "the cure" is taken. The waters are recommended for rheumatic illnesses, and the Roman-Irish baths here are open to the public.

Whether or not you try the bathing, take a look inside at the Jugendstil decor. Mixed bathing is Monday and Thursday 1-10pm, Friday 9am-10pm and Saturday and Sunday 10am-7pm. Women-only days are Tuesday 9am-10pm and Thursday 9am-1pm. Men's day is Wednesday 9am-10pm. The bathing is nude. Three hours is the recommended time for the complete bathing experience, and instructions are posted in English.

Heading back toward the middle of town, you will come across the Schiffchen (Little Ship). It is a block of buildings shaped like a ship, bordered by Grabenstraße and Wagemann. Like most of the town, it has been renovated and now contains traditional wine and beer bars and shops.

Turn down Marktstraße, which brings you opposite the **Rathaus** (City Hall). There is a small brewery in the *Ratskeller* restaurant downstairs. The brewmaster is a member of the Binding family (who owns one of Frankfurt's breweries.) He estranged himself from his family when they became "too commercial" and he set up shop, surprisingly, in one of Germany's premier wine regions.

The white ducal palace **Landtag** (Parliament buildings), dominates the square. Across the way is the Old City Hall, the

oldest building in Wiesbaden, dating from the seventeenth century. These days, it is used only for weddings.

Each Wednesday and Saturday a market takes place on the square. It is not cheap, but the food is fresh, top quality, and artistically displayed. The Wine Festival and Christmas Market take place here.

The towering red-brick **Marktkirche** (Market Church) is the main Protestant church in town. Its Catholic counterpart facing the Luisenplatz is the **St. Bonifatiuskirche**. It replaced the original church that collapsed two years after it built in 1829.

Before you go to the Luisenplatz, wander through the pedestrian zones (*Fußgängerzonen*en). Kirchstraße is the main shopping street, and while there are stores in all price categories, Wiesbaden shops do tip toward the luxury end of the scale. There are five arcades in the center of town.

Upstairs the Friedrich Passage on Friedrichstraße is the restaurant *P&N* (for Pizza & Noodle). It is Italian and decorated in the national colors of green, red, and white. Paintings by the owner Rafael Uliano hang on the walls, an artist in the kitchen as well, and his delicious pasta and veal concoctions are real bargains.

Above Wiesbaden, perched on the side of the Neroberg, is a **Greek Orthodox Chapel**, crowned by five gold domes. It was built to house the tomb of Elizabeth, the young Duchess of Nassau, who came from Russia to marry into the royal family. She lies in white marble on a marble tomb, surrounded by the 12 apostles and watched over by marble angels.

The church is still an active parish under the bishop from nearby Darmstadt, and its Christmas and Easter services are particularly impressive. Wiesbaden has a large Russian community. Many wealthy Russians settled here when they fled the revolution.

The church nestles among dense foliage above the lovely old villas, and from here there is a panorama of the city spread out below.

The city's small vineyard is nearby on the Neroberg – there is a larger one outside town. Higher up the Neroberg is an outdoor swimming pool, the Opelbad, which merges onto a vista of vines and church spires. You can reach the pool by the Nerobergbahn, a little rack railway that runs in summer.

Another pool visitors will enjoy is the heated indoor-outdoor pool in the Aukamm section of town. Steaming water is piped, through two kilometers of pipeline, into the modern blue-roofed building from the Kochbrunnen. It is quite an experience to swim in the warm water in a snow-covered landscape.

Wiesbaden has been situated directly on the Rhine since it acquired the village of Biebrich in 1928. With the acquisition of the village came the **Biebrich Castle**, one of the best examples of baroque architecture found along the river. It was built as residence for the Dukes of Nassau. The two wings were begun in 1699 and later connected by the long central section.

The Rhine side of the castle is best viewed from a cruise ship, while the best land view is from the park. The interior cannot be visited. This is where the International Horse Show Jumping is held in spring, and there are outdoor concerts in summer. Many old trees grow in the park. A collection of its plants was sold to Frankfurt to start the Palmengarten.

Just down the road from the castle is the villa where Wagner wrote his *Rheingold*.

**Shierstein**, another suburb and former fishing village, is the site of the city yacht harbor and an old baroque church with a magnificent organ – a perfect setting for Bach concerts.

Further along is **Frauenstein Castle**. In spring, cherry trees blossom around the ruins, framing the town below. This is the best place to try the regional Rheingau wine.

Wiesbaden sits at the gateway of the Rheingau wine region, which produces some of Germany's finest Rieslings and Müller-Thurgaus. The city is also a premier producer of *sekt*, sparkling wine, Germany's equivalent of champagne. The Henkel firm's turn-of-the-century offices are a sight in themselves, and concerts are sometimes given in the marble lobby.

For information about Wiesbaden, contact the tourist office on Wilhelmstraße at the corner of Rheinstraße: Verkehrsbüro, 15 Rheinstraße, D-65185 Wiesbaden. Tel. 0611-1729780/1, fax 0611-1729799.

## Mainz

Mainz, with its 180,000 residents, is most ebullient during *Fasching*, the pre-Lent Carnival season. The Rose Monday Parade (Rosenmontagszug), which takes place the Monday before Ash Wednesday, is one of the most famous of the Rheinish Carnivals. Though its spirit is young, Mainz is a very old city.

It is across the Rhine from Wiesbaden, about 36 kilometers from Frankfurt, and can be reached by Autobahn 67 and 60, or by the S-14, and in summer by cruise ships.

Its 1,000 year-old Cathedral on the Marktplatz was the spiritual center of the Holy Roman Empire of the German Nation. The rose-red spires dominate the city and serve as a landmark to help you find your way. The city has a special way of helping you become oriented: all streets with blue nameplates are perpendicular to the river. The best way to see Mainz is to wander around at random; you will stumble upon its tiny corners and charming by-ways – the "real" side of the city. There are, however, a few highlights not to miss.

The **Dom**, St. Martin's Cathedral, was founded in 957 by Willigis, Archbishop of Mainz. It is the best of the trio of Romanesque cathedrals on the Rhine – the other two are at Worms and Speyer. (Open daily 9am-5pm.)

The oldest section of the church dates back to the fourth century, and its patron, St. Martin, stands high on the roof above the western apse. The interior has many monuments to the Archbishops, sculpted by leading artists of their day. Notice the paintings on the upper walls of the northern and southern arches, and stop at the Altar of the Virgin (1520), beside the Ketteler tomb. The West Choir stalls were carved by court cabinetmarker, Franz Hermann, in the eighteenth century. The Eastern Crypt holds a golden reliquary, containing the relics of the Mainz saints.

Walk along the Gothic cloisters, the two-story windows of which overlook the inner court. This is the site of the grave and monument of the Meistersinger Heinrich von Meissen, who was honored by the mayor of Mainz in 1323 for his songs praising women.

There is an interesting museum in the cloisters, **Bischöfliches Dom- und Diözesan-Museum** (Open Mon.-Sat. 9am-noon, and Mon.-Wed. and Friday 2-5pm.) It houses some very early treasures from the cathedral. Among them are a stone head carved by an anonymous Naumburger Meister around 1240, and an expressive sculptured stone group, *The Damned.*

In the Market Square at the cathedral stands a column of uncertain origin. It is generally believed that it was once part of the cathedral, but was removed when the ceiling was vaulted. It is called, irreverently, *phallus columnus* by the Mainzers. Some years ago, the city decided to dress it up, so a sculptor built a bronze base for it. The four corners of the base tell the history of the city – the bishop's mitre, the knight's helmet, the imperial crown and the jester's cap. The fox peeking out of the helmet is a pun on Mayor Fuchs (Fox). Carved at one corner is a Star of David and the burning Jewish ghetto.

Across the square from the cathedral is a row of lovely old buildings, each with a different facade. Restoration has been carried out methodically in Mainz. The city was heavily damaged during World War II. In the Old Town, virtually the only thing left intact after the bombing was a quarter which had been scheduled for demolition. Those buildings have now been restored.

A market takes place in the square beside the cathedral each Tuesday, Friday and Saturday morning. Nearby, at 5 Liebfrauenplatz, is the **Gutenberg Museum**, dedicated to the Mainzer who gave us print. (Open Tues.-Sat. 10am-6pm, Sun. 10am-1pm.) The museum surveys the history and process of printing, and its great treasure is a Gutenberg Bible printed in Mainz in 1452-55. Changing exhibitions are mounted.

One of the newest art treasures in Mainz is in **St. Stephan's Church**, at Stefansplatz, which has seven stained·glass windows by Marc Chagall. (Open daily 10am-noon and 2-5pm. Tours, also in English, Mon.-Fri. 2-3pm.) The deep, deep blue is electrifying, and the artist's interpretation gives new excitement to the familiar story of the Bible. Bring binoculars for close study.

The **Museum of the Central Rhineland** (Mittelrheinisches Landesmuseum), at 49-51 Große Bleiche, contains one of the best collections in the country of archeological finds from the area – and Mainz is particularly rich in Roman and Germanic artifacts. When the Hilton Hotel, at 68 Rheinstraße, was being built, a well-preserved Roman boat was unearthed. The museum also has a collection of Höchst porcelain and a number of works by important Flemish painters, including Breughel. (Open Tues.-Sun. 10am-5pm.)

The deepest sparkling-wine cellars in the world are in Mainz, in the **Kupferberg Winery**, 19 Kupferbergterrasse. Some of those cellars date from Roman times. In the middle ages, the nearby Altmünster Monastery added more cellars. Today, the cellars descend seven stories underground.

In addition to a collection of champagne glasses and Art Deco advertisments, the firm has the original tasting room of the German Wine Trade that stood at the World Exhibition in Paris in 1900. Groups can arrange English-language tours and wine tastings at the Kupferberg Sektkellerei, Tel. 06131-1051.

*Mainz is known for its rich selection of qualitative wines*

The **Mainz Wine Festival** is held on the last weekend in August and the first weekend in September in the Volkspark (People's Park). Another wonderful time to visit is during the St. John's Eve Festival in mid-June, an event which includes boat-jousting contests on the Rhine. There is a Carnival and an Open Ear Music Festival in the summer.

A good place to try the wine is the *Haus des Deutschen Weines* at 3-5 Gutenbergplatz. Some 44 wines, which you can buy by the glass, from all over Germany are on the wine list. The food is excellent and moderately priced.

The Rheingoldhalle and the City Hall are on the shore of the Rhine behind a spacious plaza. The **Rheingoldhalle** hosts conventions and concerts, and has just installed a casino to compete with its neighbor, Wiesbaden.

For information about Mainz, contact the Tourist Office, 15 Bahnhofstraße, D-55116, Mainz. Tel. 06131-286210, fax 06131-2862155.

## The Taunus

The Taunus Range, a forested massif, shields Frankfurt from cold north winds. Its highest point, the Großer Feldberg, stands 878 meters (2887 feet) tall. This is Frankfurt's playground. When smog hangs low over the city, a long line of traffic snakes into the hills, where the air is clear, and the sun quite often shines. Once a stronghold of robber barons, it now attracts those who wish to escape the confines of the city.

It can be reached by Autobahn 5 (Bad Homburg exit) or 661, U-3 to Oberursel, S-4 to Kronberg or S-3 to Bad Soden.

The Taunus stretches some 80 kilometers from Bad Nauheim to Wiesbaden on the Rhine River and has several charming spa towns, walking trails, castles, and even a reconstructed Roman fort. It is ideal for a day's outing, which can be stretched into a relaxing longer stay.

In the heart of the Taunus are a number of spas: Bad Homburg, Königstein, Bad Ems, Bad Soden, Bad Schwalbach, and Schlangenbad. They have the calming atmosphere of "cure" towns with many springs and landscaped parks.

**Bad Homburg** is a town with a population of around 50,000. The Taunus Therme spa is one of the larger spas. The casino in the Spa Park is called the "Mother of Monte Carlo" because it was founded in 1841 by the Blanc brothers, who went on to open the Monte Carlo casino in 1866. Outside, the casino it is surprisingly plain, the architecture over-shadowed by the copper-domed bathhouse at the edge of the park. There is a shuttle bus service for visitors between Frankfurt and Bad Homburg.

Fountains are scattered throughout the grounds, and you will also see a Siamese Temple and a Russian Chapel, mementoes of the visits of King Chulalongkom of Siam and Czar Nicholas of Russia. Concerts are held both indoors and outdoors at the concert hall and band shell.

Behind the cure park is the modern **Taunus Therme** (06172/40640), a pool open to the public, which has indoor and outdoor heated pools, saunas, and nudist areas.

About nine kilometers from Bad Homburg is **Saalburg**, a second-third century Roman garrison outpost, reconstructed about 1900 at the site of archeological finds. Saalburg was a part of the Limes, a long stretch of for-tifications that the Romans put up from the Danube to the Rhine. It included mounds and ditches, watchtowers, and forts, and was built to protect the triangle of land that the Romans held between those two rivers – the northern boundary of the Roman Empire.

The walls of this fort, with four gates and the spacious drill hall, have been recon-structed, along with barracks and clay-domed ovens. Remains of a bath house

*An enticing pastoral green landscape in the Taunus area*

can be seen toward the back end of the enclosure. Just behind the main gate is the **Horreum**, the granery, which has been turned into a museum. Its exhibits trace the Roman occupation, and the everyday objects, such as leather shoes and red tiles are especially interesting.

The number of wells on the premises is striking: a total of 99 have been found, the deepest one being 26 meters (app. 90 feet). Outside the walls, traces of the old Roman Road which led to Nidda (now Frankfurt-Heddernheim) can be seen. There are cellars where a village once stood, as well as the remains of a *Mansio* (inn) for traveling officials. Further away are the sanctuaries for the gods Mithras and Jupiter.

Traces of the limes can be found in many spots in the Taunus forests. Wanderers may come upon them as they follow the walking trails which criss-cross the range.

A number of trails converge at the top of the **Großer Feldberg**, the highest point in the Taunus. The gently sloping hill top, beneath the Federal Post Office's huge telecommunications tower, is a favorite place for kite flying in summer and sledding in winter. There is a lookout tower that can be climbed (167 steps), a terrace restaurant, and a Falkenhof (display of birds of prey). The **Falkenhof** has an interesting collection of eagles, falcons, owls, and vultures, and sometimes a falconer is on hand to present his predatory charges. (Closed in winter.)

The Großer Feldberg can be reached by Bus 5950 from Kronberg and Königstein and Bus 5942 from Bad Homburg and Oberursul.

**Kronberg** is a little town of half-timbered houses, restaurants, and boutiques. A typical carving over a doorway reads "Johannes Fuchs erbauet mich im Jahr Christi 1715" (Johannes Fuchs built me in A.D. 1715). A large house at 15 Schloßstraße is more florid, with a golden eagle on the door and a spy mirror at one window. Look at the old stocks in the garden behind.

The castle, **Burg Kronberg**, stands at the corner of Schloßstraße and Obere Höllegasse. Its oldest section dates from 1220. (Open daily except Mon. 9-11am and 2-3pm. Guided tours on the hour). Opening times are not always reliable.

For those who want to linger, there are plenty of small pensions and hotels, as well as the luxurious castle hotel, *Schloßhotel Kronberg*, at 25 Hainstraße. Tel. 06173-70101. This was the very first of the *Gäste im Schloß* (Guest in the Castle) hotels which are now found all over Germany and in some other European countries. After World War II the castle was taken over for a time by the U.S. Army.

Try to get a peek of the private property of the Baron Achim von Freyberg, a Frankfurt fashion designer – a real Russian tea house. It was ordered from Russia in the mid-nineteenth century, brought to Frankfurt in 2,000 numbered pieces, and reassembled at Kronberg. The intricately carved columns and fretwork gables are a fine example of Russian peasant architecture. It has been lovingly restored as a home by von Freyberg.

Between Kronberg and Königstein is the **Opel Zoo**, a wild-animal park.

At **Königstein** there is an even more impressive castle than at Kronberg. This is the second-largest castle ruin in Germany, and it gives a wonderful panoramic view of the Taunus, across to the towers of the Feldberg. A piece of another ruin, the Falkenstein, can be seen peeking around the top of the hills. It can also be visited.

Königstein lacks the history of Kronberg, but has a newer charm along its little pedestrian zone and in its Kurpark. The *Park Café* looks as if it tried to be a Swiss chalet, but got mixed up with a Black Forest farm house. There is live music at noon Sunday, and the lunch menu is moderately priced.

## A Cruise on the Rhine

Between Easter and mid-October, the cruise season, you can choose river trips lasting from half a day to a week. Local excursion boats, from every Rhine port, make short excursions. The only Rhine trip from Frankfurt without changing boats is run by the White Fleet of the *KD Köln-Düsseldorfer* German Rhine Line. The line has regularly scheduled trips from Basel, Switzerland, to Rotterdam, The Netherlands. A Christmas and New Year's cruise and a floating wine seminar in autumn are also part of the KD cruise program.

Information is available from KD in Frankfurt at Am Eisernersteg, Tel. 285728, fax 282420.

The ship leaves Frankfurt from the Eiserner Steg on the Right Bank of the Main River, cruising through the locks at Schwanheim, and entering the Rhine near Mainz and Wiesbaden. It continues over the loveliest stretch of the Rhine, between Mainz and Koblenz, to Cologne.

If you have only one day to spend, you can take a cruise along any stretch of the river and return by train. KD tickets can be used on the railway – just get the ticket validated for the train at the KD ticket office when you leave the ship.

We will concentrate on the Rhine cruise between Mainz and Koblenz.

The Main joins the Rhine about 500 kilometers from the Rhine's source. It is easy to know just where on the river you are – each kilometer is marked in huge numbers and the quarter-kilometers are marked on smaller signs.

Heading north, the Mainz is to your left and Wiesbaden to your right. Church spires

compete with industrial smokestacks on both sides of the river, but at Wiesbaden-Biebrich you get a taste of things to come with an excellent view of Biebrich Castle, a lovely baroque palace. The river turns, and soon charming wine villages appear with regularity. This is one of the best wine-producing areas of Germany – the vines get the double warmth of the sun, directly reflected from the water.

Boats dock at most of the picturesque villages, and for those who have time, it is fun to make several stops, wandering among the half-timbered houses and trying out the local wine pubs, and then catching the next boat.

Rüdesheim is the best-known of these villages among English-speaking people, but other charming places are Eltville, Oestrich-Winkel, Assmansshausen, St. Goarshausen, Bignen, Bacharach, and St. Goar.

At this stretch of the river a castle sits atop almost every hill. Some are ruins, some have been converted into hotels, and many contain museums. Cloisters, too, dot the hillsides.

### EBERBACH

Above Eltville is the former Cistercian Abbey of **Eberbach**, where the film *The Name of the Rose* was shot. Eberbach is now the seat for the administration of the Hesse State Wine Domains, and is also one of the most impressive European works of monastic architecture. The monks who founded Eberbach in 1135 had an extensive knowledge of agriculture, and employed local lay brothers in their vineyards, as well as working there themselves. The monastery flourished until the Peasant's Revolt in 1525, when its famous "great barrel" was emptied and many of its books and works of art were destroyed.

It was revived in the 1700s and the buildings were embellished with baroque decoration. In 1803 the princely House of Nassau took over the estates. Later the buildings were used as a prison, insane asylum, and military convalescent home. Restoration began in 1926.

What the visitor sees today is the medieval structure with a few later enhancements. The outer wall, dating from the twelfth and thirteenth centuries, still stands. The church is severely Romanesque; its only remaining works of art are a few intriguing tombs.

The tomb of the Archbishop of Mainz, Gerlach von Nassau, shows a narrow extended figure lying in a slight curve. A later Archbishop, Adolph II of Nassau (died 1475), is shown in his death throes.

The wine cellar is not open to the public, but the Lay Brothers' Refectory, dating from about 1200, contains a dozen ancient wine presses.

Each spring and autumn auctions of the Rheingau wines take place in Eberbach (open to the public). A vinterns' thanksgiving service is held after the harvest each year and the monastery is open year-round.

Near Bingen, the river turns again, forcing its way through a narrow canyon at the Binger Loch. Just before the narrows stands the **Mäuturm** on a little island. The name of the tower comes from the word *Maut*, or toll. No doubt, you will be told the legend of the Archibishop of Mainz who was locked up in the tower to be eaten by mice as punishment for having a group of starving people burned to death.

In former days, heavy tolls were collected here for use of the river. This spot was excellent for strongmen who could control river traffic, because the stretch between Rüdesheim and Lorch could not be crossed by ships. Goods had to be portaged around the shallows until a channel was cut in the late Middle Ages.

### RÜDESHEIM

**Rüdesheim** established its fame 200 years ago when the first rugged tourists went by mule from Rüdesheim into the Niederwald, the forest on the slopes above the town. A century has passed since Germania, sometimes called Germany's Statue of Liberty, was built in that forest and began attracting visitors, who either climbed up or took a rack railway to the monument.

Now a cable car takes visitors on the gentle climb, over the vineyards to Germania. But though Germania gave birth to tourism in Rüdesheim, thousands of people now come just to see the town.

What is the secret of this attraction? Thomas Jefferson visited the area, was treated to a wine tasting, and declared that *Rüdesheimer Hinterhaus* was his favorite wine. In addition, some of today's visitors are American GIs who bring their wives to show them where they were in the early 1950s.

Of course at that time there was no Drosselgasse, the little street lined with restaurants and wine taverns, booming with *oompah* music – the street that tourists consider typically Old Germany. Anyone looking for trendy souvenirs will find them here – the

shops sell everything from Hummel figurines to cuckoo clocks. But there is much more to the town.

Explore its wine museum and vineyards, visit the Asbach brandy distillery, delight in the mechanical musical instruments of Siegfried's Mechanisches Musikkabinett, climb up to Germania and stop for a look at the falconry there. Take a pony or carriage ride at the Pony Hof above town, and pay a visit to the Benedictine Cloister of St. Hildegard, surrounded by vineyards.

Rüdesheim is spread out along the river, and the Rheinstraße, where terrace cafés look out over the busy Rhine.

Wine is the lifeblood of the town. Legend has it that Charlemagne ordered that grapes be planted here after he looked across the river from his stronghold and noticed that the snow melted first on the slopes above Rüdesheim.

The wine grown now belongs to the famous Rheingau region and is mostly white *Riesling*, although the village Assmannshausen is well-known for its *Späteburgunder* red wine. The wines can be tasted at *Straußwirtschaften* (wine taverns), which display green wreaths to indicate that they

sell their own wine. They are closed during the autumn harvest season. The town has a big wine festival in August and a festival of the new wine, *Federweisser*, when the harvest ends.

The wine museum, in the old Brömserburg castle, has an impressive collection of 1,200 drinking vessels, dating from the eighth century BC, as well as a number of old wine presses. It is open daily from mid-March until November. One hotel, the *Lindenwirt*, in the middle of town, has even arranged six big wine barrels with bunks and bathrooms – you can rent a barrel for two for around 100 DM per night.

The town has paved a Wine Learning Trail, a gentle ramble through the vineyards behind town, with the various stages of wine growing explained on signs made from barrel-bottoms. A leaflet in English guides you over the trail (available at the tourist office). The trail is open year-round, except before the harvest when the grapes need peace and quiet.

Many people climb through the vineyards to Germania or take the cable car from Rüdesheim or Assmannshausen.

**Germania** symbolizes German unity, commemorating the country's unification in 1871. A monument of a woman with the 6-meter (20-foot) waist is holding aloft the Emperor's crown with one hand and with the other a sword. The front of the monument is spanned by a remarkable bronze relief depicting the kings, counts, and dukes of the German nation – in life size. On the sides stand the angels of war and peace, and another relief depicting Father Rhine and his Daughter Mosel.

More than 50 kilometers of walking trails around the monument are marked. There are a number of lookout points in the forest, built by the Count of Ostein in the days when ornamental "follies" were the rage.

Information about Rüdesheim is available from the Tourist Office, 16 Rheinstraße, D-65385 Rüdesheim, Germany. Tel. 06722-2962, fax 06722-3485. All the staff speaks English.

### ON FROM RÜDESHEIM

On a hill above Rüdesheim stands the ruin of **Ehrenfels Castle**, used by the Archbishops of Mainz to control river traffic below.

As you continue along the Rhine, in close succession on the left bank stand **Rheinstein Castle**, another toll station now containing a large collection of arms and armor, and *Reichenstein Castle*, now a hotel, also containing an interesting collection of arms.

Next comes **Sooneck Castle**, then **Stahleck**. The first dates from the eleventh century and was restored for the last time in the 1840s. The second is a ruin, with a youth hostel built inside.

On a little island in the middle of the river here is one of the most picturesque sites on the entire Rhine. A little fortress stands on the island, looking something like a ship. It is the **Pfalzgrafenstein**, usually called the *Pfalz bei Kaub*. It was built in 1326 and enlarged about 300 years later. It, too, was a toll station.

On the right bank you see *Gutenfels*, dating from the thirteenth century and restored as a hotel. On the left bank, we approach *Schönburg*, another ruin restored as a hotel. It dates from the tenth century.

The row of rocks in the river is called **Die**

**Sieben Jungfrauen** (The Seven Virgins). Legend has it that seven maidens were turned to stone when they spurned the advances of the river god.

The best-known legend of the Rhine is the *Loreley*. A song, describing the legend, is played on the loudspeaker as the boat approaches the huge slate stab which rises beside the river. It tells of the nymph who lured sailors to their deaths on the treacherous rocks with her singing. Her bronze statue sits on a point in the river.

Still on the right bank, facing each other from their hilltops, are the Katz and Maus Castles (Cat and Mouse Castles). **Katz Castle** was built in 1370, destroyed by the French in 1806 and reconstructed at the end of the nineteenth century. It is a holiday house for the Federal Finance Ministry. **Maus Castle** (actually Burg Thurnberg) is about the same age and was privately restored, though visitors are admitted.

Between the two lie **St. Goarshausen** on the right and **St. Goar** on the left, connected by a ferry.

Above St. Goar stands the **Rheinfels**, once one of the mightiest castles on the entire Rhine. It was destroyed by the French in 1791, and its stones were used in building the citadel of Ehrenbreitstein in Koblenz. Today it houses a hotel and museum.

On the right you approach **Liebeneck**, a baroque castle, and **Marksburg**, the only fortress on the Rhine which was not at one time destroyed. If you can stop to visit just one castle, this should be the one. It dates from the thirteenth century and has a good museum of weapons.

Next comes **Castle Lahneck**, also dating from the thirteenth century, but destroyed by the French. It stands where the Lahn River joins the Rhine and overlooks **Stolzenfels**

**Castle**. A neo-Gothic structure built in the mid-nineteenth century, this castle is on the site of an older castle, whose remains were incorporated into this one.

## KOBLENZ

**Koblenz**, with its 107,000 residents, is the first sizable city since Wiesbaden and Mainz. It stands where the Mosel River joins the Rhine, and here the picturesque stretch of castles ends.

Look to the right at **Ehrenbreitstein**. This fortress was only built in 1816, and by the time it was finished, it was almost obsolete. It is second in size only to Gibraltar. It could be captured only by siege or treachery but was abandoned before it was very old. A chairlift takes visitors to the top where there is a wonderful view of the mountains of the Eifel and Hunsrück. The garrison houses the **Museum of the Rhine**, the **Provincial Museum**, and the **German Film Archives**, (it is deemed to be the safest place to store highly flammable celluloid). A 200-bed youth hostel is situated in one corner of the fortress.

Koblenz is a charming place with a large *Weindorf* (wine village) on the river bank. The village of wine restaurants was built for the 1925 German Wine Exhibition and is a replica of a vintner's village. It is open year-round, except November. From Easter until the end of October there is music, dancing, and entertainment every evening. It is a 10-minute walk from the railway station and boat docks.

The high point of the Koblenz calendar is "Rhine in Flames," always the second Saturday in August. Seventy boats carry merrymakers along the 17-kilometer stretch from Braubach/Spay to Koblenz. Castles, fortresses, and citadels are floodlit, and the fest goes on along the shores of every village. At about 11pm, the boats arrive at

Koblenz. The lights go out and the fireworks begin. One of the best places on shore to watch is the man-made Deutsches Eck (German Corner), a park which juts into a point where the Rhine and Mosel Rivers meet.

Information about Koblenz is available from the Tourist Office, Post Box 2080, D-56020 Koblenz, Germany. Tel. 0261-33134 or 0261-31304, fax 0261-1293800.

*An excursion boat will take you for a cruise along the Rhine*

After Koblenz, the river banks become more and more industrialized, and the castles more sparse. The approach to Cologne gives a view of the Cathedral, somewhat marred by industrial buildings.

# "MUSTS"

For those who have very limited time in Frankfurt and who are not sure of which sites to choose first, we have listed a few attractions that are "musts" for any visitor.

**Römer and its Kaisersaal**: This is the exquisite Imperial Hall in Römer, the City Hall, situated on the Römerberg (see p. 57).

**Hauptwache, Freßgass', Alte Oper**: Wine or dine in one of the charming restaurants, pubs, and shops in this area. Walk along Steinweg to the Goetheplatz, cross the street to the Freßgass', which is lined with shops and restaurants and leads directly to the magnificent **Alte Oper** (see p. 89-91).

**Alt-Sachsenhausen:** The restored area of bars, restaurants, and applewine pubs in a pedestrian zone (see p. 67).

**Museum Row:** Extending along Schaumainkai between the Museum of Applied Arts at No. 17 and the Liebieghaus (Museum of Sculpture) at No. 71. Includes seven museums in a riverside park setting. The others are the Ethnological Museum, the German Film Museum, the German Museum of Architecture, the German Postal Museum and the Städel (see p. 73-81).

*The Dom Cathedral with its huge Gothic tower*

**Palmengarten:** Admission gates at 61 Siesmayerstraße, and on Palmengartenstraße and Zeppelinallee. A large park containing greenhouses of sub-tropical and tropical plants (see p. 117).

**Goethehaus:** 23 Großer Hirschgraben. Furnished in eighteenth-century style, the house exhibits objects from Goethe's era and houses archives (see p. 94).

**Dom Cathedral:** On the Römerberg. Built in 1315, the electoral and coronation church of the Holy Roman Empire of the German Nation. Archeological excavations in the Historical Garden (see p. 55).

**Senckenberg Museum of Natural History:** 25 Senckenberganlage. Germany's largest natural history museum, with an impressive exhibit of dinosaurs and giant whale skeletons (see p. 103).

**Main River Cruise:** For a different perspective of the city take one of the excursion ships along the waterfront. They run from Easter until autumn and dock near the Eiserner Steg at the Mainkai (see p. 50, 155).

**Henninger Tower:** 60-64 Hainer Weg. The grain elevator of the Henninger Brewery is a landmark in Sachsenhausen. Revolving restaurant, brewery museum, and observation platform (see p. 70).

*The impressive
Alte Oper*

# MAKING THE MOST OF YOUR STAY

## Wining and Dining

Although a cosmopolitan city, Frankfurt provides a relatively bleak restaurant scene. Many of the best restaurants are found in the better hotels. While you can get excellent international cuisine, too many restaurants offer elegance without atmosphere. Unless you are willing to pay top price for gourmet food, it is best to try the many good ethnic restaurants or the applewine pubs. Here you can enjoy the typical Frankfurt dish of *Rippchen* (pork ribs) and Sauerkraut, washed down with the tart drink that is the city's specialty.

**Applewine** – *Ebbelwei*, made from apples by the same process that grapes are made into wine, is similar to hard cider. The tartness may take some getting used to, though it comes in several stages of maturation. Sachsenhausen is a popular area for apple wine pubs.

*Süßer* is sweet apple juice suitable for children. *Rausch*er is the fermentation state, *Heller* is ready to drink, and *Alter* is last year's fully mature wine.

A fresh evergreen wreath over the door indicates that a pub has new wine. The wine is served in a quilted-pattern tumbler, usually at long tables where you can feel free to join the crowd – just ask if the seat is free. These pubs also serve hearty food in large portions, including several kinds of sausages (frankfurters, schnitzels, and *Handkäs mit Musik* (another Frankfurt specialty), and a curd cheese marinated in onions and vinegar.

Frankfurt's other specialty is *grüne Soss*e – green sauce – made from seven herbs, a tasty sort of homemade mayonnaise. Those tissue-wrapped packages you see at the vegetable stands contain the raw ingredients: parsley, sorrel, dill, burnet, borage, chervil, and chives.

Seasonal dishes will appear on many of the menus too. In autumn the restaurants may have a *Wild-Karte*, a game menu, including venison, rabbit, and wild duck. Asparagus and strawberries come in June. At this time, spargel, a large, white asparagus is typically served with boiled potatoes and either drawn butter or hollandaise sauce. As side dishes, you may get ham, schnitzel, or salmon.

Pubs often offer *Schlachtplatte*, a selection of freshly-made sausages, on the day a pig is slaughtered.

Frankfurt has two breweries – Henninger and Binding – and its own vineyards (including a tiny one within the city). The most popular types of beer are

167

*Pils* (pilsner) and *Export*. Also available is the strong, dark *Alt*, or *Bock* beers or the light, fizzy *Weizen* (wheat) beers. It takes seven minutes to pour a *Pils* properly, so be prepared to wait. It arrives with a creamy head spilling over the side of the glass. *Bier vom Faß* means *"on tap"*; *Flaschenbier* is "bottled".

Frankfurt's in-city vineyard, on the Lohrberger Hang, produces just enough wine for every 100th resident to have a liter bottle – that's about 6,000 liters a year. It is a dry *Riesling*. This tiny plot, called the "Door to the Rheingau," is the eastern most vineyard of that famous wine region that produces some of the best wine in Germany.

The city also owns a large vineyard in the Rheingau, at Hochheim am Main, near where the river converges with the Rhine. The vineyard enjoys a climate warmed by the winds from North Africa. It also primarily produces *Riesling*. The city's *Weingut* sales outlet is in the Römer, at 2 Limpurger-gasse. (Open Mon.-Fri. 7:30am-4pm. Tel. 2123680). A sample of Lohrberger is included in the six-bottle gift package. The vineyard sales outlet is in Hochheim, at 11 Aichgasse. (Open Mon.-Fri. 8am-noon. Both shops close at Christmas and for summer vacation. Groups tours can be arranged for wine tastings and a tour of the vineyards at Hochheim. Tel. 06146-2374.)

Restaurants post the *Speisekarte* (menu) out front. Many restaurants have daily specials (*Stammessen*), especially at lunchtime, and some have a *Stammtisch* (table) reserved for regular customers.

Cafés and *Konditoreien* display tempting arrays of sweets (*Kuchen Torten*), which you can order with large globs of whipped cream called *Schlagsahne*. Cafés usually serve breakfast until late morning and light lunches, but most close early in the evening. Most serve *Bethmännche*n – marzipan balls decorated with three slivers of almond. It is believed that they represent the sons of local philanthropist and banker Simon Moritz von Bethmann.

With the exception of the winter season, many Italian Eis Cafés can be found. They offer a rainbow collection of ices

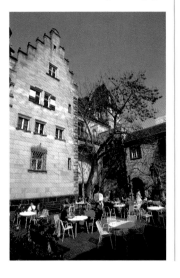

and ice-creams to eat in a cone, as well as ice-cream based concoctions with fruit, liqueur, nuts, chocolate sauce, and whipped cream.

If you prefer to munch instead of lunch, try one of the soft, fat pretzels sold by street vendors. At an *Imbiß or Schnellimbiß* you can get steaming hot wursts. Whenever a festival is in progress, you will find stands selling *Kartoffelpuffer* – hot potato pancakes with applesauce. In winter, roasted chestnuts make for a tempting snack. Some restaurants have *Straßenverkauf* windows where you can order take aways (*Zum Mitnehmen*).

There are wonderful delicatessens and butcher shops along the Freßgass' and in the Schweizerstraße. Many butcher shops – *Metzgerei* – sell hot food at lunch time and have standing room for quick snacks. There are plenty of pizzerias and burger bars as well.

A few of the best delicatessens include *Plöger Delikatesse*n on the Freßgass', *Bechtoldt* on Kaiserhofstraße, an*d Meyer Metzgerei* at 42 Schweizer-straße, which caters.

Note that restaurants are listed in the telephone book under *Gaststätte*n. The word "restau-rant" is not attached to all eating places. Establishments may be called *Lokal*, *Stube*, or *Stubb*. In good weather, both cafés and restaurants are likely to have open-air eating areas.

Here is a selection of reliable restaurants in and near Frank-furt. It is advisable to telephone before you go, since many restaurants close for a day or two each week.

### FOOD WITH A VIEW

*Boothaus am Eisernen Steg:* boat anchored at the Eiserner Steg, drinks only.

*China Restaurant Nizza:* 17 Untermainkai, roof terrace. Tel. 235185.

*Gerbermühle*: 105 Deutschher-rnufer at Gerbermühl-Werft (Wharf). Tel. 655091. Some people say this is place in town for the best applewine. It does taste especially good while being sipped on the lovely lawn that runs down to the river.

*Henninger Turm:* 60-64 Hainer Weg. Tel. 6063500. Revolving restaurant atop the brewery's grain elevator. Take a table beside the window in the revolving section. There is also a Brewery Museum and an outdoor observation platform.

*M.S. Woden Restaurant:* Boat anchored at the Eiserner Steg.

*Rotisserie 5 Continents:* Airport terminal B on the sightseeing terrace level. Tel. 6903444. Watch the planes take off and land.

### APPLEWINE PUBS
*Apfelwein-Klaus:* 10 Meisen-

gasse. Tel. 282864. Sidewalk tables. A popular spot with the locals.

*Buchscheer:* 17 Schwarz-steinkautweg. Tel. 635121. Use the pleasant garden for an enjoyable outdoor drink when the weather is good.

*Dauth-Schneider:* 5-7 Neuer Wall. Tel. 613533. Always full. Lively atmosphere.

*Eichkatzerl:* 29 Dreieichstraße. Tel. 617480. Traditional family establishment. Pork chops and hot headcheese.

*Fichtekränzi*: 5 Wallstraße. Tel. 612778. Warm and hospitable. Home made cider, pork chops, and liver are the specialities.

*Germania:* 16 Textorstraße. Tel. 613336. Complete with old-style wooden tables in the courtyards.

*Zum Grauen Bock:* 30 Große Rittergasse. Tel. 618026. Good food and drink. Popular live music.

*Hinnerkopp:* 53-59 Große Rittergasse. Tel. 615025. Applewine matured in home-made oak barrels.

*Klaane Sachsehäuser*: 11 Neuer Wall. Tel. 615983. Old-fashioned family establishment.

*Lorsbacher Tal:* 49 Große Rittergasse. Tel. 616459. Very popular. Sit on a long wooden table in a courtyard behind an art nouveau gate.

*Wagner:* 71 Schweizer Straße. Tel. 612565. Packed to the rafters on weekends. The best applewine pub in town.

*Zum Gemalten Haus:* 67 Schweizer Straße. Tel. 614559. Note the rustic paintings on the outer walls.

## RESTAURANTS SERVING GERMAN SPECIALITIES

*Börsenkeller*: 11 Schillerstraße. Tel. 281115, 293144. Popular for business lunches.

*Frankenkeller:* 69 Hedderich-straße. Tel. 282516. A mixture of Franken and French cook-ing, with an extensive wine list.

*Frankfurter Stubb:* 33 Beth-mannstraße. Tel. 215679 or 210251. Located in the cellar in the *Hotel Frankfurter Hof.* Regional specialities.

*Goetheplatz:* 4 Goetheplatz. Tel. 282516. The hearty soups are especially good.

*Gutsschänke Neuhof*: Take highway A661, exit Dreieich, 13 kilometers from Frankfurt. Tel. 06102-3214. Outside town, set in an old estate with walking and riding paths, a bakery, and gift shop. Worth an afternoon outing just for the coffee and home baked cakes.

*Haus Wertheym:* 1 Fahrtor on the Römerberg, Tel. 281432. Inter-esting decor and *Eisbock* beer.

*Maaschanz:* 75 Färberstraße. Tel. 622886. A cozy place near the river, serving zucchini and excellent roast lamb.

*Obere Schweinstiege:* In the City Forest at Obere Schweinstiege. Tel. 684888. Lovely setting beside the pond.

*Onkel Max am Salzhaus:* 4 Am Salzhaus. Tel. 288588. A pub, terrace, and picnic tables all in one large room. The *Eintopf* (a hearty soup) is good and the service congenial.

## INTERNATIONAL RESTAURANTS

*Die Gans:* 76 Schweizer Straße. Tel. 615075. Good food in Sachsenhausen.

*Geheimratsstube:* (in the *CP Plaza Hotel*), 2 Hamburger Allee. Tel. 770721. Gourmet cuisine at the fairgrounds.

*Hessischer Hof:* 40 Friedrich-Ebert-Anlage. Tel. 75400 or 7540929. Excellent food. The collection of Sevres porcelain is a feast for the eyes.

*Humperdinck:* 95 Grüneburg-weg. Tel. 722122. One of the best restaurants in town. Beautiful decor and outstanding cuisine.

*InterCity-Restaurant:* Second floor of the main railway station. Good food, fast service.

*Jacques Offenbach:* in the Alte Oper. Tel. 1340380. A good choice before or after a concert.

*La Truffe:* (in the *Parkhotel*), 28-38 Wiesenhüttenplatz. Tel. 26978830. At its best during the week.

*Papillon:* (at the *Sheraton Hotel-Airport*). Tel. 69770. Gourmet cuisine. Extraordinary food at extraordinary prices.

*PX:* 4 Feldbergstraße. Tel. 724444. Italian nouvelle cuisine in a glitzy setting.

*Mövenpick-Baron de la Mouette*: 2 Opernplatz. Tel. 20680. Much better than the usual chain restaurant. Big brunch buffet on Sundays.

*Français:* (in *Steigenberger Frankfurter Hof*),1 Am Kaiser-platz. Tel. 21502. Another of the city's best.

## VEGETARIAN

*Eden:* 4 Rahmhofstraße (near the stock exchange). Tel. 283189. Good authentic vegetarian cuisine.

## BISTROS

*Bistrot 77:* 1-3 Ziegelhütten-weg. Tel. 614040. One of the best eating establishments in Frankfurt.

*Cafe-Bistro Empor:* 8 Schneck-enhof Straße. Tel. 617502. Full of yuppies.

*Le Midi:* 47 Liebigstraße. Tel. 721438. French-style atmosphere, with delicious French cuisine.

## JAPANESE
*Kabuki*: 5-9 Kirchnerstraße. Tel. 282594.

## CHINESE
*China Restaurant:* at the Airport, Tel. 69070939. or 6902510.

*Panda:* 10 Düsseldorferstraße. Tel. 251290. An interesting menu with authentic specialities from North and South China.

*Tse-Yang:* 67 Kaiserstraße. Tel. 232541. Elegant, expensive, and busy.

## ITALIAN
*Da Angelo:* 12 Elsheimer Tel. 721801. Near the Alte Oper, a favorite for after the concert.

*Da Bruno:* 15 Elbestraße. Tel. 235680. or 233416. Old time Italian cuisine.

*La Galleria:* 2 Theaterplatz. (in the BfG skyscraper) Tel. 235680 Reasonably good food, but expensive. Extremely popular with businesspeople.

*La Salsiccia:* 11c Leipziger Straße (on the edge of the shopping arcade). Tel. 703431. Try the daily specials in the display case.

*Pizzeria Mammamia:* 7 Steinweg (Passage). Tel. 288494. A friendly restaurant in a cellar. Tasty and not expensive. Also open for lunch. Recommended.

*Ristorante Incontro:* 64 Kettenhofweg. Tel. 725881. Elegant and expensive.

## THAI
*Bangkok:* 17 Sandweg, near the zoo. Tel. 491360. Good food. Mainly a young crowd.

*Siam:* 8 Am Hauptbahnhof. Tel. 253444. Ignore the appearance and concentrate on the delicious exotic food.

## VIETNAMESE
*Grüner Bambus*: 61 Ostend Straße. Tel. 446434. Excellent little restaurant. One of the best finds in Frankfurt.

# Wine Cellars
The interiors are often as interesting as the mix of people who come here. Typical cellars have brick arches and rustic furnishings; some have open fireplaces. All have large wine lists.

*Blaubart:* 18 Kaiserhofstraße. Tel. 282229. Old vaulted cellar, wooden tables, and candlelight.

*Dünker*: 265 Bergerstraße. Tel. 451993. Sells wine by the carton only.

*Erdbeerstübchen*: 18 Kaiserhofstraße. Tel. 281518.

*Die Fabrik:* 1 Mittlerer Hasenpfad. Tel. 624406. Set in a nineteenth-century brick factory. Good steaks and vintage wines.

*Franziskaner Weinkeller:* 10 Feldbergstraße. Tel. 723220.

*Der Keller:* 3-5 Gartenstraße. Tel. 627333. Wine, beer, and light Alsation style meals.

*Künstlerkeller:* 2 Seckbächer Gasse. Tel. 292242. Established in thirteenth century by mendicant friars.

*Sachs:* 119-125 Darmstädter Landstraße. Tel. 615002. A class of its own, the restaurant was conceived as a mini-Frankfurt built in the cavernous cellars of the Henninger Brewery. It is filled with copies of real cafés and bars, but they do not have a chance to develop real character because of the rock music that blares into every corner. Although expensive, it is frequented by the young.

## Beer, Bars and Clubs

The *Lokal*, *Stubb*, *Pilsstube*, or *Kneipe* are likely to have a large selection of beer. Breweries usually set up a bar or restaurant for a cut of the profits, and most beer houses serve a respectable selection. A few specialize in variety. It would be impossible to list all the beer bars in Frankfurt, because almost every restaurant serves beer and wine and many of them have large bars and tables for drinkers only. The following is a list of the most popular ones:

*Biergarten:* 73 Schweizer Straße. Tel. 612815.

*Palais des Bieres:* 77 Schweizer Straße. Tel. 627282. Sidewalk tables. Parisian style.

*Weihenstephan:* 3 Rathenauplatz. Tel. 283868. Serves beer brewed by "the oldest brewery in the world".

## Entertainment

There is always something to do in Frankfurt. Entertainment listings can be found in the local newspaper, in the biweekly guide *Frankfurter Woche*, and in the alternative magazines *Pflaster Strand* or *A-Z*. The Tourist Office and the city information office have listings of concerts, theater, festivals, and sports events, and Ads are posted on the street and in the U-Bahn stations.

### THEATERS

For theater events Tel. 11517. Unless you are an opera fan or speak German, you may wish to skip the theater scene.

One English-language theater is located at the *Café Theater* (45 Hamburger Allee. Tel. 777466), which schedules performances regularly. The *Frankfurt Playhouse* also stages English-language shows. This little theater is for the U.S. military community stationed here. The theater is located at 56 Hansaallee and is not included in city-wide theatrical billings. Tel. 1518326 or Tel. 2562434 for advance bookings.

## Concerts

Concerts are held in halls, museums, and at open-air concert sites. The Palmengarten is a popular setting for jazz concerts. For more informations on concerts, Tel. 11517. The major concert halls include the following:

*Alte Oper Frankfurt:* Opernplatz. Tel. 13400.
*Festhalle:* (at the Fairgrounds) 1 Ludwig-Erhard-Anlage. Tel. 75750.
*Jahrhunderthalle Höchst*: Pfaffenwiese. Tel. 3601240.

Tickets can be purchased at the box offices and at ticket agencies. Box offices open one hour before show time. Below is a list of several ticket agencies:

*Concert-Poster and Kartenvorkverkauf:* 37 Berlinerstraße. Tel. 293131.

*Frankfurter Kunstgemeinde:* 2 Eschersheimer Landstraße. Tel. 1545145.

*Kartenvorverkauf:* Am Liebfrauenberg, 52-54 Liebfrauenberg. Tel. 293131.

*Colorful Frankfurt*

*Ticket Agency* (Konzert/Theaterkasse): In Hertie Department Store. Tel. 294848.

## Cinemas

Frankfurt has about 80 cinemas, a great number of them located around the Hauptwache. Most films in Germany are dubbed, but there are two English-language cinemas, and the repertory cinemas sometimes show films in the original language, or with English subtitles.

**English-language cinemas**
*Airport Cinema:* Terminal C, Level O. Tel. 6904645.
*Turmpalast:* Am Eschersheimer Tor. Tel. 281787.

**Repertory cinemas**
*Cinema Studios:* 177 Bergerstraße. Tel. 456405.
*Harmonie:* 54 Dreieichstraße. Tel. 613550.
*Kommunales Kino*: 41 Schaumainkai. Tel. 2128830. In the Film Museum.
*Orfeo:* Hamburger Allee. Tel. 702218.

## Music

### JAZZ

Jazz is alive and well in Frankfurt and number of clubs provide everything from Dixieland to jazz-fusion. Trombonist Albert Mengelsdorf isa Frankfurter, and he often plays in town. The following is a list of some popular jazz clubs:

*Der Jazzkeller:* 18a Kleine Bockenheimer Straße. Tel.

288537. A Free jazz stronghold in the Nazi era.

*Jazzhaus:* 12 Kleine Bockenheimer Straße. Tel. 287194. Tiny two-story establishment in a historic-landmark building. Recorded music. If you can squeeze in upstairs, your drinks are hauled up in a basket.

*Jazz im Schlachthof:* 36 Deutschherrnufer. Swing, Dixieland, rock, and old-time music on Sundays from 11am.

*Jazzkneipe:* 70 Berliner Straße. Tel. 287173. Live music from 10pm.

*Jazz Life Podium:* 22 Kleine Rittergasse. Tel. 626346.

*Niddapark-Terrassen:* 52 Woogstraße. Tel. 520522. New Orleans to country-and-western.

*Opernkeller:* 0pernplatz (in the Alte Oper). Tel. 1340320. Dixieland and swing every Friday night.

## LIVE MUSIC

Live jazz, rock, and country-western clubs include:

*Batschkapp:* 24 Maybachstraße. Tel. 531037. International music scene. The blaring music is hard on the ears.

*Brotfabrik:* 2-4 Bachmannstraße. Tel. 7894340. Salsa-disco in a former bakery.

*Klimperkiste:* 1 Affentorplatz.

Tel. 617032. Blues, rock, soul, and golden oldies.

*Sinkkasten:* 9 Brönnerstraße. Tel. 280385. Varied activities in pleasant atmosphere.

*Spritzehaus:* 41 Große Rittergasse. Tel. 614336. Rock and oldies.

## DISCOS

Frankfurt has its share of dance clubs and the scene changes frequently. Your best bet is to ask around when you arrive to learn which discos are the most popular.

*Blue Infinitum:* 2-10 Hamburger Allee (at the *CP Plaza Hotel*). Tel. 79552315 or 770721. Dance beneath the twinkling stars.

*Dorian Gray:* At the Airport, O-Level. Tel. 6902212. A little bit of everything, from video to dance. Entrance only to those with the right appearance. Very in, very expensive.

*Le Jardin:* 6 Kaiserhofstraße. Tel. 288956. Chic young scene. Right of admission reserved.

*Montgolfiere:* 16 Unterschweinstiege (in the *Steigenberger Airport Hotel).* Tel. 69750. Cocktails and jazz.

*Music-Hall:* 74-80 Voltastraße. Tel. 779041. Live and taped performance of latest and hottest international hits.

*Nouvelle:* 2 Gallusanlage. Tel. 252218. A young, noisy crowd, but still a lot of fun.

*UNO:* 9 Biebergasse. Tel. 287697. Admittance gained only by the select.

*Vogue:* 14 Junghofstraße. Tel. 282233. Chic scene. Italian restaurant and midnight buffets.

## Casinos

Frankfurt has no casinos of its own, but two in nearby cities offer shuttle bus service:

*Casino Wiesbaden:* 1 Kurhausplatz, Wiesbaden, Tel. 0611-536100. Open daily 3pm-3am. Roulette, American Roulette, Black Jack, Restaurant and bar. From 2pm-midnight: Slot machines (Poker, Black Jack and Roulette automats), Derby, Super Jackpot. Individual transfer service.

*Casino Bad Homburg:* In Kurpark, Bad Homburg, Tel. 06172-17010. Restaurant and bar, hourly bus transfers between 3pm-2am from Hauptbahnhof (South Side), Manheimer Straße. Bus ticket credited towards casino entrance fee.

## Sports

Whether you prefer to be a spectator or participate actively, Frankfurt can provide plenty of opportunities for the sports enthusiast. With its eye on the Olympics in the year 2004, the city is planning to build Europe's largest sports hall.

The city has its own **soccer** team and league matches are now played in the *Waldstadion* (Forest Stadium) in the south side of the city. Tickets and information are available from Eintracht Frankfurt e.V., located at Am 25 Erlenbruch 25, tel. 419179.

**Horse racing** takes place at the *Rennbahn* in Niederrad on most Sundays from May through November. Take Straßenbahn Line 15 or Bus no. 61. Advance tickets are available from Rennbahn Sekretariat, 125 Schwartzwaldstraße, tel. 677018.

**Outdoor pools** are open May to September if weather permits.

*Gartenhallenbad Rebstock:* 7 August-Euler-Straße. Open Monday 2-10pm, Tues. and Thur. 9am-8pm, other days 9am-10pm. The complex has a

50-meter warm-water pool, a pool for the handicapped, gym room, heated outdoor pool, solarium, saunas, restaurant, cafe, sports shop, and conference rooms.

There is a combination **squash** and **bowling** center, with sauna, beer bar, grill restaurant, and natural-food restaurant near the "Office City" in Niederrad. Pueblo, 114 Goldsteinstraße, tel. 6666111.

## Festivals and Fairs

There are countless small festivals and fairs that take place in and around the city. It should not be difficult to stumble upon one, but you can ask about them at any tourist office. Some events warrant special mention.

The Carnival season, that period of wild partying before Lent, is called *Fastnacht* or *Fasching* in Germany. The Carnival celebrations in Frankfurt are not as well known as those in neighboring Mainz or in Cologne, or as steeped in pagan tradition as the events to the south in Rottweil, but the city is still exciting when festivals or fairs are under way.

Private parties and costume balls start with the official beginning of *Fasching* – the 11th minute of the 11th hour of the 11th day of the 11th month

*At the Messe – a giant statue greets the visitors*

– at 11:11am on November 11 – but things really get rolling from the Thursday before Ash Wednesday. The big *Fastnacht* parade through downtown is on Sunday. Do not be surprised to see costumed celebrants on the streets during those days – or office workers and shop clerks wearing startling make-up and glitter in their hair.

Twice a year, in spring and fall, Frankfurt has its *Dippemess* at the Festplatz on the Ratsweg. What began as a pottery fair has expanded to include booths selling just about everything. Plenty of food and carnival rides are also available.

The Festival of Roses and Lights takes place in June in

the Palmengarten. Visitors will admire the many varieties of roses and the illuminated fountain. There is a spectacular fireworks program as well.

*Waldtag* takes place the Tuesday after Whitsun. Shops close early for Frankfurt's *National Day* and the people go out to the City Forest to walk, picnic, or enjoy the small carnival set up there.

Open-air theater, music, and special theater programs (including tent-theaters in the parks) are highlights of the cultural events that take place during the "Summertime" fest that runs from June through August. "Festive June" also takes place at the Alte Oper.

The Castle Festival in Höchst is in the early summer. The Main Festival, which has its origins as a fisherman's festival, takes place along the river in July or August and includes boatmen's jousting. In August the applewine Brunnenfest is held in Sachsenhausen. That month or in September the Open-Air Market in Bergen takes place.

The year ends with the Christmas Market set up during the Advent season on the Römerberg. Carved wooden creches and Christmas tree ornaments, toys, roast chestnuts, and hot spiced wine (called *Glühwein*) are sold from the stalls.

The New Year – *Sylvester* – is brought in with parties and plenty of fireworks.

## Where to Shop for What

Frankfurt's commercial tradition is particularly evident in its shopping districts. Here you can buy anything from trendy jewelry hawked by sidewalk vendors to *haute couture* in exquisite boutiques. Shop hours are strictly controlled by law. Regular opening hours are Monday-Friday 9am-6:30pm, though some stores may not open until 10am and some take long lunch breaks. Shops close at 2pm Saturday, except the first Saturday of the month and every Saturday in Advent, when they can remain open until 6pm.

The following is a list of the main downtown shopping areas:

*On the move*

*Zeil:* Pedestrian zone with shoe stores, furniture stores, and clothing stores. The Kleinmarkthalle, a covered food and flower market, is nearby on Hasengasse.

*Schillerstraße*: Pedestrian zone between the Hauptwache and Eschenheimer Turm. Boutiques and home-furnishing stores.

*Steinweg:* Pedestrian zone between Hauptwache and the Goetheplatz. Jewelry, clothes, books and perfume.

*Goethestraße*: Between Goetheplatz and the Alte Oper. A street of exclusive clothing and jewelry shops.

*Freßgass'*: Pedestrian zone between Goetheplatz and the Alte Oper. The cafés, wine shops, delis and, restaurants are interspersed with clothing, gift, and antiques shops.

*Kaiserstraße*: A long street from the Rossmarkt (near the Hauptwache) to the main railway station. Leather and shoe shops, jewelry, carpet and clothing stores.

*Ladengalerie am Theater:* A shopping center in the BfG skyscraper.

Toward the station, the shops become less expensive and include a number of sex shops and shops selling electronic equipment. However, the city is planning to renovate the area, and establish banks, businesses, and living quarters there.

*Zeilgalerie – a chic modern shopping arcade*

Good shopping areas away from the center of the city include the Schweizer Straße and the streets radiating out from Schweizerplatz in Sachsenhausen, the area around the Bockenheimerwarte, especially Leipzigerstraße, in Bockenheim, and along the Bergerstraße in Bornheim.

Germany is not a bargain-hunter's paradise, but it is respected for its quality products. When making a large purchase, it may be worth your time and effort to get a rebate on the value-added tax (*MWT*) which is included in the price of all items.

### DEPARTMENT STORES

The large department stores along the Zeil are *Kaufhof, Kaufhalle, Hertie, Peek & Cloppenberg, M. Schneider.*

179

*Kaufhof – one of the large department stores along the Zeil*

## BOOKS

Many book shops can be found in and around the Hauptwache. The shops often have a selection of English-language paperbacks. The largest selections of English-language books can be found at the following addresses:

*The American Book Center:* 36 Jahnstraße.
*British Bookshops:* On Börsenstraße.
*The Hiller Stores:* At the airport and main railway station.
*Frauenbuchladen:* 27 Kiesstraße. For feminist literature.

Foreign-language books can be found at the following addresses:

*Librairie Française*: 6-8 Kirchnerstraße.
*O.C.S.:* 1-7 Große Gallusstraße. For Japanese literature.
*Dr. G. Zambon:* 24 Leipzigerstraße. For Italian, Spanish, Portuguese, and Turkish Books.

## COMPACT DISCS

German recordings are excellent. Among the best are *Deutsche Grammophon* for classical and *ECM* (the brainchild of Manfred Eicher) for modern jazz. Rock can be found everywhere and there are also many recordings of oompah bands.

*Noten Haus W.E. Fuchs:* 70 Bleichstraße. Discs are available, but the store is best-known for its variety of sheet music and song books, including old books.

*Phonohaus:* 7 Rossmarkt. Pop downstairs, classical, jazz and ethnic upstairs.

*Zweitausendeins:* 10 Kornmarkt. Often has bargains.

## LEATHER

Neighboring Offenbach is center of the leather industry. In addition, many factories have shops in Frankfurt. Most specialize in either clothing or handbags and luggage, though some have both. Department stores and certain boutiques also carry leather goods.

*Gold-Pfeil:* 22 Kaiserstraße, at the airport, and in the *Intercontinental Hotel:* Outstanding selection of handbags, luggage, and briefcases from its Offenbach factory.

*Leder-Stoll:* 50 Schäfergasse, 68 Schweizer Straße, and 24 Leipzigerstraße.

*Leder-Vater:* 18 Kaiserstraße

and 6 Katharinenpforte. Sells jackets, pants and skirts.

## GLOVES
*Roeckl:* 7 Kaiserstraße.
*E. Wahl:* 16 Große Eschenheimer Straße.

## CLOTHING
Germans still wear traditional costume and you will see men in *Lederhosen* (short leather pants), though not as much in Frankfurt as in southern Germany. Some of the best and the most practical of traditional clothing to take back home are *loden* coats, jackets, capes and suits. The cloth is usually green, but can be found in navy blue and gray. It is water-resistant and very warm. *Loden* can be found in sports shops, especially hunting and fishing supply stores.

## FOLK COSTUME
*Liesel Steinmetz:* 14 Rathenauplatz (near the Hauptwache).

## DESIGNER CLOTHES
Germans have the reputation of dressing in a dull way, and while some clothing is less-than-daring, many German designers keep pace with the best of Europe. French and Italian labels are popular. The designer shops *Krizia, Guy Laroche, Gianni Versace*, and others are on Goethestraße.

Tailor shops for made-to-order clothing are called *Maßschneiderei*.

Other designer shops include:

*Dieter Gundlach:* 13 Börsenplatz. For men's clothing.
*Atelier Bechtloff:* 65 Mörfelder Landstraße. Makes shirts and blouses.
*Küchel:* 11 Bleidenstraße. For men's and women's clothing.

## WOMEN'S CLOTHES
*Alpha-exclusiv:* 54 Schweizer Straße.
*Annabel of Königstein*: 9 Goethestraße.
*Claudia Adolff:* 6 Große Bockenheimer Straße.
*Cris Bittong:* 19 Oppenheimer Landstraße.
*Escada:* 13 Goethestraße.
*Eve:* 46 Freßgass'.
*Freyberg:* 52 Diesterwegplatz (across from the Südbahnhof).
*Riffel:* 25 Goethestraße.

## MEN'S CLOTHES
*Annas:* 31 Goethestraße, 36 Kaiserstraße and 39 Große Eschenheimer Straße.
*Sacco & Coxini:* 71 Schweizer Straße.
*Uli Knecht:* 35 Goethestraße.

## MEN'S AND WOMEN'S CLOTHES
*Lantana:* 15 Kaiserhofstraße.
*Möller & Schaar*: 35 Goethestraße and 4 Steinweg.

## CHILDREN'S CLOTHES
*Bambini:* 4 Schneckenhofstraße (exclusive fashion).
*Kinderhaus Pfüller*: 12 Goethestraße.

*Trude Hahn:* 50 Beth-
mannstraße.

## LINGERIE
*Lingerie von Hayn:* 43
Schweizer Straße.
*Madame-Wäsche*: 31 Goethes-
traße.

## HOSIERY
*Fogal:* 4 Goethestraße. The
Fogal brand is also carried by
other hosiery shops.

## UMBRELLAS
*E. Wahl:* 16 Große Eschenheimer Straße.
*Schirm Klippel:* 6 Katharinenpforte.

# Cosmetics and perfumes
The big chain is *Douglas*,
found all over town.
Cosmetics can also be purchased at a *Drogerie*, which is
very much an American-style
drugstore but only sells cosmetics, toiletries and related items.

## SPORTS AND CAMPING GEAR
The sports shops cater to the
ski crowd in winter and the
tennis crowd in summer. Some
specialize in windsurfing,
skating, and other sports.

*Angler Zentrale F. Bissinger:* 2
Ziegelgasse. Everything for the
fisherman.

*Bedo-Sports:* 4 Frankensteiner
Platz. For walking and running
shoes.

*Fink:* 9 Rossmarkt. A department store for sports.

*Intergolf:* 18 Holzgraben. For
golf equipment.

*Sport Berntheusel:* 65 Hamburger Allee. For ice and roller
skates.

*Sport Maritim:* 5-7 Eschersheimer Landstraße. For sailing,
diving, surfing gear, as well as
for tennis gear and walking
shoes.

*Sporthaus Maul:* 14-16 Neue
Mainzerstraße. A sports department store.

*Supertramp:* 26 Homburger
Straße. For trekking, wilder-
ness wandering, and mountain
sports.

*Tanz & Tennis Lady:* 2 Theaterplatz. For tennis and ballet.

*White Sports:* 82-84 Mainzer
Landstraße. For tennis.

## TOYS
Adults are as likely as children
to be impressed in German toy
shops. Wooden toys, stuffed
toys, superb model trains – anything a child would want is here.
*Steiff* cuddly animals are very
popular, although expensive.

*Behle Spiel & Freizeit:* 107
Zeil, 18 Kaiserstraße and 312
Eschersheimer Landstraße. For
almost everything.

*Gerd Riedel:* 26 Friesengasse. For model trains.

*Hanne Kley:* 12 Rossmarkt and 366 Eschersheimer Landstraße. For wooden toys and furniture.

*Hobby Haus:* 36 Braubachstraße. For model trains.

*Modellbahn-Treff:* 41a Königsteiner Straße. For model trains.

*Puppenklinik:* 32 Friedberger Anlage. For doll repair.

*Spielwaren Ade:* 15 Neue Kräme. For almost everything.

*Das Spielzimmer:* 32 Große Friedberger Straße. For wooden toys and children's furniture.

## CAMERAS AND ELECTRONICS

A number of shops advertising "Tax Free" are grouped around the Hauptbahnhof and the Rossmarkt. Collectors can find used and antique cameras and photo equipment at *Heinz Bodenheimer*, 26 Alte Gasse and *Photo Brell*, 62 Kaiserstraße (in the Passage).

## ANTIQUES

Many antiques shops can be found around the Römerberg, especially along Braubachstraße and neighboring streets. Here are just a few specialized shops.

*Antik S. Urlass:* 3 Ziegelgasse. Art Deco and Bauhaus.

*Antik Wolf Hoedt:* 1 Mittlerer Hasenpfad. Specialist in Biedermeier.
*Antiquitäten-Stör:* 7-9 Fahrgasse. Specialist in dolls and toys.
*Buttlar & Kann Antiquitäten:* Rossmarkt. For furniture.
*Claudia's Antikladen:* 47 Hochstraße. Jugendstil and Art Deco.
*Lothar E. Bogdanski:* Freßgass'. Rare carpets.
*R. Lang:* 1 Börsenplatz. Mainly art.
*Vinariae:* Rossmarkt. Wine rarities and corkscrews.

## ART GALLERIES

*Galerie Brumme:* 34 Braubachstraße. Old graphics and maps.

*Galerie Grüner Panther:* 20 Eckenheimer Landstraße. A combination Irish pub and gallery.

*Galerie Woeller Pacquet:* 10 Schneckenhofstraße. Modern art.

*Kunsthandlung H.H. Rumbler:* Börsenplatz and traditional art.

*La Galeria:* Sandgasse. Jewelry, silk, and glass.

*Margot Ostheimer:* 33 Braubachstraße. Naive and folk art. Do not miss the creches at Christmas or the eggs at Easter.

*Vonderbank:* 11 Goethestraße. Modern art and posters.

## KITCHEN AND HOUSEHOLD ITEMS

*Lorey:* 16 Schillerstraße. For designer garlic presses, copper and stainless steel utensils, and superb cake pans.

## MISCELLANEOUS

*Rosenthal Studio-Haus Gilbert:* 10 Friedenstraße. For Rosenthal china.

*Tiffany Art:* Sandgasse. Recommended for stained glass.

*Comic:* 18 Berlinerstraße. For comic books, posters, and cards.

*Katzen und Kunst:* 24 Braubachstraße. For anything related to cats.

*A+L Pokal Trophäen*: Schwertfegergässchen (on the Römerberg). For trophies.

*Strunkmann & Meister:* 17 Kaiserstraße. For bath and kitchen linens.

*Neumann Stempel:* 16 Stiftstraße. For engraving, metal signs and rubber stamps.

*Bürstenhaus Drossner*: 9-17 Stiftstraße. For brushes, sponges, and everything for bath or cleaning.

## FOR IMPORTED ARTICLES

*Art España:* 56 Bethmannstraße. Spanish furnishings.

*Schweden Krone:* 39 Stiftstraße. For Scandinavian gift items, food, and drink, including a stand-up snack bar.

*Vieille Provence:* 10 Römerberg. Products from the French Provence plus *Liberty* scarves from England.

## THE FLEA MARKET

Every Saturday morning, the flea market (*Flohmarkt*) sets up at the old *Schlachthof* (slaughterhouse) in Sachsenhausen. It was moved there a few years ago from the Schaumainkai along the Main River. There are plenty of old clothes. The patient browser may sometimes find a real antique bargain.

## Important Phone Numbers

### EMERGENCIES

Police: 110.
Fire: 112.
Ambulance: 490001.
Emergency doctor: 79502200 or 19292.
Emergency dentist: 6607271.
Pharmacy: 11500.
Helicopter Rescue: 441033.
Hospital (Uniklinik): 63011.
Red Cross Accident Assistance: 233364.

### INFORMATION

Airport Information: 69030511.
Train Information: 19419.

Phone numbers (national): 01188.
Phone numbers (international): 00118.
Telex, Teletex, Datex: 1172.
Telegrams (German): 1131.
Telegrams (foreign language): 1133.
Time signal: 1191
Lost and found offices: 7500-2403, 7500-2404.

## AUTOMOBILE BREAKDOWN SERVICES

ACE: Wilhelm-Leuschner-Straße 69-77, Tel. 19261.
ADAC: Schumannstraße 4-6, Tel. 74300.

AvD: Lyoner Straße 16, Tel. 6606600.

## AIRLINES (*LUFTVERKEHRS-GESELLSCHAFTEN*)

*British Airways*: Tel. 250121.
*Deutsche Lufthansa*: Tel. 230621.
*TWA*: Tel. 770601.

## CONSULATES

Great Britain: Consulate General, 42 Bockenheimer Landstraße. Tel. 170002-0.

U.S.A.: Consulate General, 21 Siesmayerstraße. Tel. 75350.

## Vocabulary

| ENGLISH | GERMAN | ENGLISH | GERMAN |
|---|---|---|---|
| good morning | *guten Morgen* | port, quai | *Hafen, Kaj* |
| hello | *hallo* | slow | *langsam* |
| goodbye | *auf Wiedersehen* | fast | *schnell* |
| good evening | *guten Abend* | gas | *Benzin* |
| good night | *gute Nacht* | gas station | *Tankstelle* |
| please | *bitte* | | |
| thank you | *danke* | hotel | *Hotel* |
| pardon, excuse | *Entschuldigung* | hostel | *Herberge* |
| yes | *ja* | room | *Zimmer* |
| no | *nein* | toilets | *Toilette* |
| what...? | *was...?* | bath, shower | *Bad, Dusche* |
| when...? | *wann...?* | restaurant | *Restaurant* |
| where...? | *wo...?* | café | *Café* |
| there is... | *es gibt...* | table | *Tisch* |
| there is not... | *es gibt nicht...* | chair | *Stuhl* |
| how are you? | *wie geht es Ihnen?* | | |
| | | waiter | *Kellner* |
| far | *weit* | water | *Wasser* |
| near | *nahe* | bread | *Brot* |
| big, large | *groß* | drink | *Getränk* |
| small | *klein* | menu | *Speisekarte* |
| new | *neu* | hot | *heiß* |
| old | *alt* | cold | *kalt* |
| right | *rechts* | soup | *Suppe* |
| left | *links* | meat | *Fleisch* |
| first | *zuerst, erster* | salad | *Salat* |
| last | *zuletzt, letzter* | bill | *Rechnung* |
| open | *offen* | receipt | *Beleg* |
| closed | *geschlossen* | | |
| entrance | *Eingang* | cinema | *Kino* |
| exit | *Ausgang* | theater | *Theater* |
| | | pharmacy | *Apotheke* |
| bus | *Bus* | shop, store | *Laden, Geschäft* |
| bus station | *Bushaltestelle* | news-stand | *Kiosk* |
| train | *Zug* | post office | *Posamt* |
| subway, | *Untergrund-* | hospital | *Krankenhaus* |
| underground | *bahn* | police | *Polizei* |
| railway station | *Bahnhof* | embassy | *Botschaft* |
| ticket | *Fahrkarte* | | |
| taxi | *Taxi* | market, bazaar | *Markt* |
| car | *Auto* | how much | *Wieviel* |
| plane | *Flugzeug* | does it cost? | *kostet das?* |
| airport | *Flughafen* | expensive | *teuer* |
| boat, ship | *Boat, Schiff* | cheap | *billig* |

| ENGLISH | GERMAN | ENGLISH | GERMAN |
|---------|--------|---------|--------|
| road, highway | Straße, Autobahn | November | November |
| street | Straße | December | Dezember |
| avenue | Avenue | | |
| square | Platz | 1 | eins |
| alley | kleine Straße | 2 | zwei |
| esplanade | Esplanade | 3 | drei |
| bridge | Brücke | 4 | vier |
| monument | Denkmal | 5 | fünf |
| fountain | Brunnen | 6 | sechs |
| church | Kirche | 7 | sieben |
| palace | Palast | 8 | acht |
| castle | Burg | 9 | neun |
| town, city | Stadt | 10 | zehn |
| village | Dorf | 11 | elf |
| museum | Museum | 12 | zwölf |
| park | Park | 13 | dreizehn |
| | | 14 | vierzehn |
| east | Osten | 15 | fünfzehn |
| north | Norden | 16 | sechzehn |
| west | Westen | 17 | siebzehn |
| south | Süden | 18 | achtzehn |
| valley | Tal | 19 | neunzehn |
| mountain | Berg | 20 | zwanzig |
| range | Bergkette | 21 | einundzwanzig |
| hill | Hügel | 30 | dreißig |
| forest | Wald | 31 | einunddreißig |
| river | Fluß | 40 | vierzig |
| | | 50 | fünfzig |
| Sunday | Sonntag | 60 | sechzig |
| Monday | Montag | 70 | siebzig |
| Tuesday | Dienstag | 80 | achtzig |
| Wednesday | Mittwoch | 90 | neunzig |
| Thursday | Donnerstag | 100 | hundert |
| Friday | Freitag | 101 | hundert und eins |
| Saturday | Samstag | 110 | hundert und zehn |
| | | 200 | zweihundert |
| January | Januar | 300 | dreihundert |
| February | Februar | 400 | vierhundert |
| March | März | 500 | fünfhundert |
| April | April | 600 | sechshundert |
| May | Mai | 700 | siebenhundert |
| June | Juni | 800 | achthundert |
| July | Juli | 900 | neunhundert |
| August | August | 1000 | tausend |
| September | September | 2000 | zwei tausend |
| October | Oktober | million | eine Million |

# INDEX

# INDEX

# QUESTIONNAIRE

In our efforts to keep up with the pace and pulse of Frankfurt, we kindly ask your cooperation in sharing with us any information which you may have as well as your comments. We would greatly appreciate your completing and returning the following questionnaire. Feel free to add additional pages.

Our many thanks!

To: Inbal Travel Information (1983) Ltd.
18 Hayetzira St.
Ramat Gan 52521
Israel

Name: _____

Address: _____

Occupation: _____

Date of visit: _____

Purpose of trip (vacation, business, etc.): _____

Comments/Information: _____

_____

_____

_____

_____

_____

_____

**INBAL Travel Information Ltd.**
P.O.B 1870 Ramat Gan
ISRAEL 52117